IF I CANOE IT, SO CANOE!

ELIZABETH KRANZ

Tellwell Talent
www.tellwell.ca

ISBN
978-0-2288-8951-9 (Paperback)

Get Out!
Be Amazed At The
Art Of The Creator

Elizabeth Kranz

Gratitude

A huge hug and thanks to my talented husband, Doug, for all his editing help and encouragement.

Thanks to all my kids for all their love and support.

Thanks to my daughter April for her artistry within the book.

Instagram: @apirljensenart   apriljensenart@gmail.com

Thanks to all my friends and family for reading many emails with my stories. Thanks for all your kind words and for cheering me on.

The First Nations Peoples of Canada, who first travelled all over their massive, beautiful country by paddling a canoe in millions of waterways, inspired the call of the wild within me, a love for our wonderful wilderness and all our amazing fellow creatures.

Esther Keyser (1915 – 2005), the first woman to guide others by canoe into Algonquin Park's interior, awoke my passion for paddling into the wilderness with the book she and her son, John, co-authored, "Paddle My Own Canoe."

Kevin Callen has written many books that are so helpful and have motivated me as well. Check out all his entertaining and informative YouTube videos.

Bill Mason (1929 – 1988) Bill's art, books, award-winning movies, documentaries, and teaching films inspired many to venture into the wilderness to see the artistry and wonders of God in His creation.

Bill's friend and Pastor, Bill Duffy, said, "One of the things that greatly impressed me about Bill Mason is what one might call his "theology of creation.", which is just a way of describing his great love for God's world. He respected it; he appreciated it; he sensed he was a steward in it. He had such a great love for God's creation because he **knew** the God of creation. That was the key. …. And he could preach that. It came through in every aspect of his being. He was like Jerimiah; his faith was like fire in his bones."

Let me take you on a journey from vacationing by car and staying in the comfort of a cabin to paddling your own canoe far into the wilderness and sleeping in a hammock. Let me share with you the wonder of all the surprising, astounding beauty that will surround you. Come and experience the calming silence, the rejuvenation of being free of walls and barriers, to live surrounded by creation. Be filled with profound peace while the rhythmic paddling on crystal clear waters brings you back into harmony with life and closer to the Creator.

"For nature is part of the glorious fullness
of God's creation
no less than man.
I look around me at the colours,
the textures, the designs - - -
It's like being in an art gallery.
God is the artist."

Bill Mason in *Waterwalker*

Table of Contents

Welcome

What is your favourite kind of vacation? As a child, my parents took me travelling from our small farm north of Toronto to stay in various cabins or cottages around Ontario, including Parry Sound, Bracebridge, Huntsville, and Manitoulin Island.

As newlyweds, Doug and I travelled west across Canada, camping in a borrowed, old, mouldy canvas tent.

Vacations changed again as our children arrived, and we bought a small cottage near the southeast side of Algonquin Park. I taught them all to swim and paddle a canoe when they were young. We hiked and biked, and I tried to instill a love for all life and the wilderness.

Way back in the day, my oldest son asked if he could join his friends for a wilderness canoe trip. This question awakened my own youthful dreams. Of course, I excitedly gave him my permission and helped him plan and pack, even though my friend Cathy thought it would be too dangerous for a group of fourteen-year-olds to trek into the wilderness without adult leadership. My son knew well how to paddle a canoe and swim. At least two of the other teens had been canoe camping. It would be impossible for them to get lost as they paddled for only two days down the Little Bonnechere River to where we would meet them at the beach on the big Round Lake.

I felt no fear nor worry for them, only huge excitement and envy. Maybe someday I could go on my own wilderness canoe trip—some day.

Well, it took another twenty years before I got the chance. Finally, I could actually travel by canoe to find campsites in the beautiful Algonquin Park's interior wilderness.

Of course, our family had camped every summer in campgrounds across Canada, first in a borrowed tent. Then we upgraded to a tent trailer that fit our five children. However, the kids could not stand Dad's snoring, so I would make up a cozy bed in the back of the van every night. Poor dear. We even tried glamping in a secondhand RV when we took the kids on one big trip to Disney World in Florida during one March break.

Once the kids were grown, we downsized again to a tiny ultra-light A-frame pop-up trailer. Every time my husband sits in it, he says, "I love this thing."

One summer, we took a long trip with our tiny trailer all the way from our home in Ontario to Whitehorse, Yukon, and Yellowknife, Northwest Territories. On our drive home, my husband, Doug, asked me, "If you had the choice of all the places we have visited this summer, where would you like to live?"

I immediately responded, "Yellowknife."

He chose Whitehorse. So, I guess it is good that we must stay together in our tiny cottage, now home, in Ontario.

The more rugged canoe camping, further into the wilderness, has now become my passion. I will bring anyone who will join me in this adventure. But only a few will come. Will you?

My TV-addicted, computer-geek husband graciously lets me drag him on some trips. Poor dear. He must give up so much: TV, computer, cell phone, comfy bed, cushy chairs, and a secure shelter from wind, weather, and mosquitoes. He cannot swim. Although he would never mention it, I know that all windy, wavy conditions probably terrify him, stuck in a narrow canoe on a big, deep lake. But he bravely fights fear, thunderstorms, extreme heat, chilly nights, and mosquitoes just to help me live my passion for the wilderness.

He even fights his fear of bears. He had to buy and read, from cover to cover, the book *Bear Attacks in Canada*. Poor dear.

I, on the other hand, have no fears. I am not afraid of the dark or bugs or spiders or snakes or bats or bears. Humans and cars are far more dangerous than anything in the wilderness.

I am not afraid, but I am prepared and careful. I always bring a first aid kit. Everyone on any of my camping trips must wear a whistle at all times.

I am an excellent swimmer and am not able to sink. And as far as the danger from humans? I have a black belt in Judo. No fear. No worries. Only massive enjoyment in my canoe, surrounded by wilderness.

Recently Doug surprised me with a solo canoe. I can finally go on canoe trips by myself. I can pack up all my gear in one large pack and head off into the wilderness without the concern of Doug missing his tech or his comforts. I can rough it guilt-free.

Of course, many fearful friends questioned my sanity and even begged me not to go alone. Doug has solved the problem of his fears of me going on solo trips by supplying me with a satellite phone, and I can assure him daily that I am alive and well.

I have one question. Why did I not do this sooner? Seventy arrived too quickly, so I know you are thinking, "Solo canoe trips **at your age?**"

I wish to share some of my Algonquin Park adventures with you. I wish to share my love for God's peaceful, rejuvenating creation. Please realize that we share this planet with many other creatures. The wilderness is their home. Respect them. Respect their home. Realize that we can share our bench by the fireside with an ant, a spider, or a toad. Realize and respect that we need them all to survive. Be amazed by the surrounding spectacular beauty. See how artfully creative our awesome Creator is.

I must begin this book with this next story of someone who inspired generations to follow him into this wonderful wilderness.

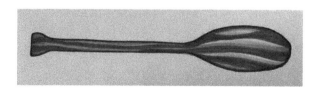

Murder Mystery in Algonquin Park

Unbelievable! How could something so horrible happen in such a peaceful paradise? A place that breathes tranquillity, emanating from a multitude of majestic tall trees, a myriad of wildlife, large and small, and a plethora of plumage, all living within this almost eight thousand square kilometres of pristine, green wilderness with high hills, swampy bogs, and thousands of sparkling clear waterways. It's so hard to believe that such a violent act could occur here, in this serene haven that inspired such beautiful art from such a talented young man.

In 1912 a tall, dark-haired, handsome stranger came to Canoe Lake and fell in love. Although a refined city boy, he quickly became obsessively in love with this wilderness called Algonquin Park. Soon he became a skilled canoeist. Inevitably, he became quite enamoured with a lovely young lady whose cottage perched on the shores of the pretty Canoe Lake.

Tom's love for the area inspired him to paint. His love for Winnie may have been what instigated his mysterious murder.

The town of Mowat, at the top of Canoe Lake, with its train station, lumber company, school, hospital and two hotels, is now gone. All that remains is the enduring, vibrant paintings of Tom Thomson and the compelling beauty of this part of God's country.

This artist came, out of curiosity, those many years ago. He came as a tourist. The call of the wild claimed him, the local culture enveloped him, and the breathtaking wilderness beauty captivated him. The city boy soon became a skilled wilderness outdoorsman. He explored and sketched, and painted many views of this vast park.

He returned each year. Employed as a fishing guide, he could share his love of this place with others by gliding quietly through the clear waters of these picturesque lakes and rivers, spying on loons, beaver, deer, moose, and the spectacular changing autumn leaves.

Visitors came by train to drink in the beauty, to be amazed at the variety of life and colour, massive moose and delicately detailed butterflies, towering green pines, tiny purple toadstools, three-hundred-foot red rock cliff walls, and soft, oh so soft, lime green mosses hiding under a canopy of enormous hemlock trees. People came to relax, paddle innumerable waterways, lay on the soft white beaches, dive from the high

9

rocks, and swim in the clean, refreshing lakes. They came for recreation and rejuvenation. They came for the healing of mind and body by the peace and fragrant, fresh air. They found indescribable beauty. Tom found a way to describe and share it through his inspirational art.

Each year Tom came, spending more and more time in the park, sketching the multitude of awe-inspiring views. Winters were spent in his Toronto city apartment, transforming these sketches into wonderful oil masterpieces while he longed to return to his loves, the wilderness and Winnie Trainer.

In 1916 his empty, up-ended canoe was found floating near the west side of Canoe Lake, close to the cottage of his rival. Eight days later, his body surfaced, floating bloated near the lake's center. Did an accident shorten his life or a vile act of premeditated homicide?

How could violence be conceived in such a peaceful sanctuary, a place with the power to revive, a place filled with the miracles of creation? Who would kill such a talented young man?

So much time has passed, and still, no one knows for sure.

Did the owner of the lodge kill him in a sudden fit of rage over a financial dispute? Or did jealousy of Tom's sweetheart drive a rival suitor to plan and wait for the opportune moment to murder him? No real investigation took place, and no one was charged or arrested.

I can't comprehend how violence could be contemplated in an environment that inspires and rejuvenates.

One hundred years ago, the tiny town at the north end of Canoe Lake hummed with activity. Nothing remains of all those buildings, now vanished back into the forest. Nothing remains but a large stone memorial for the man with so much creative talent.

So many years have buried the truth. The wilderness has reclaimed all this history. Theories have been considered, stories written, and even plays depict what may have happened, but the facts have long since turned to dust.

The only evidence of the amazing talent of Tom Thomson lives on in his beautiful art. His oil paintings show the many faces of the wilderness: lake scenes, waterfronts, canoes, log jams, a stark white tent in a dense forest, a lake covered in white caps fringed by hills of lively fall brilliance, a crimson sunset, dark waters of a stormy day, a snow-covered birch forest, the fantastic wild colours of autumn, the magical aurora borealis and a lone pine tree deformed by the harsh west wind. The art of Tom Thomson may be collected in calendars, books, and framed prints. Much of his work can be viewed in an art gallery in Algonquin Park today. See how well he conveyed his passion for this peaceful haven. See how his art inspired other artists.

Tourists come to Algonquin Park by car now, not by train. One major road runs through the southern section, past the art gallery, Canoe Lake restaurant and gift store, and a vast variety of hiking and biking trails, rock cuts, bogs, rivers, lakes, campgrounds, a logging museum, an outdoor theatre, a lodge, cabins, kids' camps, and a fascinating visitors' center.

On spring mornings, you must be careful, have your camera in hand and be ready to pull over and stop. You never know around which curve in the road a massive moose may surprise you.

You will certainly want to pull over to take many pictures in the fall. If you don't have the pictures to prove the scenery, no one will believe you when you try to explain how incredibly fantastic the colourful fall forest can be.

But engage your four-way flashers, pull far off the road, and be careful of traffic since this is a major highway used not only by campers but large transport trucks in a hurry to their destinations.

The greater part of the park, the vast wilderness interior, is only accessible by canoe. Here one can travel back in time to live simply and serenely and be captivated by the same passion that engulfed a city boy many years before. Hear the same call of the wild that transformed him into an avid canoeist and explorer. Glide through the deep, clean waters as you discover the treasures that will surprise you around every twist and turn of yet another river. Be delighted by the melodies of the pretty songbirds and awed by the intricate patterns of a butterfly. Witness a regal loon spreading his broad wings over the water's mirror surface. Be serenaded by a harmonious chorus of frogs as the sun sets with pinks and purples behind the darkening, dense forest. Sit by a warm campfire and listen to the eerie song of elusive wolves in the far distance. Lie back and marvel at the spectacular northern lights as their colours transform and dance across the sky, and be astounded at the innumerable, brilliant stars in the infinite, deep black of space.

Algonquin Park has it all: history, mystery, passion, and breathtaking beauty.

Within the park are hundreds of lakes. Some have children's camps and cottagers; some only see wildlife and the rare expert backwoods explorer.

12

Every summer, we must come and experience some part of the park, even if it's just to sit at the restaurant on the southern shores of Canoe Lake. From the restaurant windows, we watch the strange variety of visitors renting canoes here. Some go out for a couple of hours and have obviously never been in a canoe. We witnessed hilarious and treacherous stunts. Some circle in constant dizziness, some crash painfully into the dock, and some do not even leave the dock without almost capsizing! We try not to chuckle.

Then I envy the others who load up their canoes with supplies to last a week or two. They sit relaxed, effortlessly sliding the canoe swiftly down the long lake. We wonder which river they will follow, which portages they will take, and how far they will travel. I wonder if they, like me, would rather just stay in the park.

I guess that part of Tom's dream came true. He never had to return to the city. His monument sits high on a rocky hill overlooking the lake that he loved and came to call home.

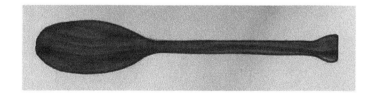

Love Affair

Will Tom Thompson's love for Algonquin Park spark a love affair for you too? Will the call of the wild lure you? We surely are compelled to return every summer. With twelve drive-in campgrounds and endless canoe routes, I will never be able to see all of the almost two million acres of incredible wilderness, crystal clear lakes and rivers whose rocky shores are hugged by aromatic cedars, towering white pines, and majestic maples.

There's so much to see and do. You could never get bored. Although, personally, I'd love to be bored if that means just sitting on the shore of one of the multitudes of beautiful lakes with nothing to do but view the incredible scenery and breathe in the peacefulness while being serenaded by a choir of birds.

We have hiked most of the over twenty-five trails, which range from wheelchair accessible to a challenging six-hour trek to the highest trail point in the park. What spectacular views!

If you're lucky, you will be privileged to see some of the countless varieties of wildlife. I have tried to learn the names and sounds of some of the many species of pretty birds. I have a special affection for toadstools. The variety of sizes, shapes and bright colours of all of God's creation constantly surprises me.

You may even have the rare opportunity to see the larger wildlife: otters, beavers, bears, deer, and moose. Such contradictory creatures, the moose! Even though they appear clumsy with their gigantic heads, long skinny legs, and knobby knees, they can gracefully and silently vanish into the dense forest without so much as a broken twig to mark their passing.

Although you may never see the elusive wolf, you may be fortunate enough to hear a lonesome, distant call some night and mistake it for a loon. But then you'll hear the response of his mate and pups until it blends into a boisterous party. Wow! Who can sleep then? You'll just have to get out of your tent, and if you weren't amazed already, you certainly would be when you see the multitude of stars.

For years the Park hosted a "Star Party." No, you wouldn't see any movie stars. But you could view spectacular deep space phenomena through telescopes of all sizes and strengths. Many amateur astronomers set up their scopes on the beach at Mew Lake campground and hope for clear skies.

In the absolute dark of night, just lay on the ground, look up and marvel at the countless pinpoints of light, the depth of infinity, and the power of the Creator. "The heavens declare the glory of God." Psalms 19:1.

Cocoon Nebula, photo taken by Doug Kranz

Doug, the astronomer, learned much about telescopes here and upgraded his scopes a few times for bigger and better varieties. It seems size does matter.

If it rains, go to the Visitor's Center to take in the film shown in the little theatre or stroll through the nature, history, and art displays. Inspect the books in the gift store and snack in the cafeteria while staring out the huge windows. Perched on a hill, this panorama view displays a lake, a meandering stream, a flat boggy area, and miles and miles of hills blanketed in green, lush trees. Search for wildlife through binoculars.

You could also take in the Logging Museum and Art Gallery. On most summer days, you can join the informative guided hikes or organized fun activities for kids. Check out the fascinating presentations, slide shows, and dramatic plays at the outdoor theatre in the evening. One year I learned that over eighty different kinds of butterflies live in the park.

Stop at the restaurant at the bottom end of Canoe Lake. Make sure you have time to visit the store, canoe rental and outfitters, and the display in the office for interior canoe trips.

Paddle a canoe the length of Canoe Lake to explore for the day, see the old cottage of Tom's sweetheart, hunt for the ruins of the old town at the top of the lake, read the tribute at the memorial to this famous artist on the top of the hill overlooking the pretty lake and imagine what it must have been like so many years ago.

Come and experience the incredible beauty, the calm serenity, and the complex diversity of colour and life that so inspired Tom Thomson and the Group of Seven. Fall in love with Algonquin Park. Feel the compelling call of the wild to return every summer to this part of God's country. Here, in Algonquin Park, feel renewed, refreshed, and amazed at the splendour of creation and the Creator.

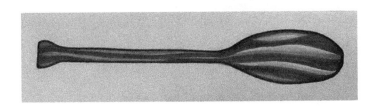

Here We Go, Ladies

Rain Lake Ranger's Cabin

My love for Algonquin Park and God's recuperative wilderness beauty drove me to drag my friends into a more remote part of the famous park.

Much planning went into getting the four of us together since we were from different parts of Ontario. Pam and Linda came from Kitchener, and Edith and I came from near Pembroke, on the Ottawa River northwest of Ottawa. We met for breakfast in Huntsville at 9 am. Then we excitedly hurried north on highway 11 to the tiny town of Kearny.

Here we had to get our permits from the park office and then our key, paddles, and life jackets for the canoes I had reserved, which waited for us at Rain Lake. Of course, the canoes and campsite had to be booked five months in advance. I told you, lots of planning.

Then came the last jaunt of our journey to Rain Lake. Soon the pavement turned into a dirt road, winding around swamps, small lakes, along rivers and streams. The dusty road shrank to a single lane. So many twists and quick turns, so close to trees and boulders, and so much loose gravel considerably slowed our progress. Luckily, we met no traffic, and no wildlife leaped out in front of us. I'm sure the three ladies wondered, "Where in the world is Liz taking us? When will we ever get there?"

Finally, the trek ended in a large, filled parking area with a few vacant campsites. It felt a bit strange to see so many vehicles but no humans. They had all gone canoeing far into the wilderness for days or even weeks of paddling, portaging, and camping.

I would never have convinced these ladies to come with me if I had suggested that plan.

When I had been here the year before, I discovered this lone, tiny old Ranger's cabin that we could rent. This year I knew I could get these ladies to come with me into Algonquin's wilderness by camping in this comparative luxury.

First, we found our canoes and took off onto the long and pretty lake. Too excited to have lunch we explored this narrow end of the lake. I must have been hungrier than the rest as I searched the forested shores for a good picnic spot. But my friends must have been captivated by the peaceful wilderness, and we paddled for quite a while.

We found a beautiful vacant campsite. Towering white pines and hemlock made a cooling canopy, and we had a soft carpet of aromatic pine needles. A huge fire pit, surrounded by a ring of fat log stools, sat in a large, level area. We had an excellent view of the lake and enjoyed our leisurely lunch.

Energized and excited, we climbed back into the canoes and set off to paddle back up the lake to claim our cabin. The wind in our faces made the return trip feel longer.

We found the cabin hidden in the tall, thick forest. This quaint log building had a tiny kitchen and eating area equipped with propane lights, a stove, a picnic table, and two small bedrooms with two cots each. An inviting screened-in porch stood attached to one side, which we had never used since no bugs tormented us. Just outside the back door sat a big stone-trimmed fire pit with a large log bench. Looking past that, we had an open view of our dock, with the two canoes and the beauty of the lake.

One mystery puzzled us. I had been informed that the cabin had a pump to access drinking water. The hunt for this elusive pump kept us busy, searching everywhere inside and outside without success. Luckily, we did have some bottled water with us; if this ran out, we could have easily filtered and boiled the lake water. No worries.

I should speak for myself, but I think we all felt like a bunch of little kids on our first day of camp, giggly and silly. We had so much to do and see and talk about. These ladies had never met, and only I had been here before.

The hot sunshine and clear waters lured us to the beach for a swim. From here, we could watch as others arrived and loaded up canoes for their adventures into the interior. The water chilled us, and the sunbaked, sandy beach warmed us.

After a simple supper, we laughed loudly while playing games. Linda displayed gigantic, colourful mugs on the table, a gift for each of us. What a fun surprise.

Later as the evening grew quieter, our campfire brightened the twilight, compelling us to tell stories. We learned a little of each of our histories. These three lovely ladies came from different backgrounds, yet we all felt very comfortable together, warmed by the glow of the fire and new caring friendships. Pam's career change from teacher to nurse kept her unbelievably busy. Edith's unique artistic talent kept her creating more extensive flower beds. Before my move away from the Kitchener area, Linda and I had taught Judo together for fifteen years.

Surrounded by giant trees, far from civilization, the night becomes extremely quiet and totally black. The stinky outhouse stood far from the cabin. Assuring them that we had nothing to fear, I still promised to walk with anyone, anytime, along the dark path to that unpleasant yet necessary spot, equipped with a flashlight, whistle, and the most essential accessory, a supply of toilet paper. It is odd that people never really sleep well the first night in a strange, new place. I will not soon forget the many trips on the well-worn path that night.

*

The day began clear and warm. Pam woke early and slipped outside, not to wake anyone else. She slid a canoe into the water and paddled around in the peaceful, still morning mist. It surprised me that we didn't all sleep late with all our many little walks in the night. The mood of eager young campers still held us. Linda spotted Pam out on the lake, and I grabbed my camera to capture that serene sight.

During a hot, healthy, yummy breakfast, we planned our day. Of course, I had to say it was yummy. I planned and made all the meals, and everyone else helped with the cleaned-up.

Before the sun began to bake the day, we paddled down the long lake. Being a fitness instructor and the only one who had done recent canoeing, I wanted to be sure the novice canoers didn't overdo it. Their memories wouldn't be fond if they ended up stiff and sore. But no one felt any tenderness from the almost two hours of paddling the previous day. Youthful excitement compelled them to insist that we head for the far end of the lake.

But I knew how long the lake extended. I knew the canoeing rule that demands there is always a strong wind on the way back. Oh well. On we went.

A scenic island sat, almost touching the far end. Tall, majestic pines towered around this ideal campsite. Fortunately, no one occupied it, so we climbed over the rocky shore to explore the ruins of a massive stone fireplace. What stories could it tell?

We had to fight the wind all the way back. We worked hard, and I'm sure we paddled hard for well over two hours that day. Instead of worrying about ill effects, my friends remained energetic kids.

After lunch, we headed down a hiking trail along an old railway line. A gorgeous butterfly welcomed us. Most of the path followed the edge of the lake, so we could watch other canoeists heading out. Easy walking until it took a detour through a bushy, musty swamp.

The ladies were concerned when we encountered fat piles of bear scat. Someone else had obviously been enjoying the luscious blackberries along this path. But the only wildlife we encountered flitted from flower to flower, and another hid in the crevasse of a gnarly tree. How did this cute little toad climb up that tree?

Edith proved to be as outgoing as my husband, her cousin. She cheerfully initiated a friendly chat with everyone we met while canoeing and walking. We met one couple on the trail. From their perspiration-covered faces, they must have been walking for some time, and their huge backpacks indicated they had been on this backpacking trail for many days. This hot day was the last leg of their trek, and it seemed to me that the pretty young lady yearned for it to be finished. But her tall, fit partner happily responded to Edith's curiosity with engaging conversation.

By the time we finished our hike, the sun had certainly warmed us, and a swim felt very refreshing. We felt no guilt that evening eating well and filling up on cookies. After lots of giggling and games, we just had to roast marshmallows around the campfire again.

In the twilight, a loon family swam into our view of the lake and serenaded us with their captivating calls.

What a full, fun day. Our cozy little bunks felt so comfortable that night, and we all slept very well.

*

Pam awoke early and took off in the canoe again, not wanting to waste our remaining fleeting time.

Instead of giddy campers bouncing with excitement, this morning found us calmer. Today, at some point, we would have to pack, clean up and leave. One wish encompassed us, more time to remain here.

Pam glided into our dock just in time for breakfast and our day's planning.

Clean-up would have to wait. We had to make time for one more excursion in the canoes. Leisurely we investigated the little swampy bays and rocky shorelines that we had dashed past the previous days.

A pair of black ducks moved out of our way into the grassy shallows. Rocks had to be avoided in some narrow, shallow areas. A silly family of merganser ducks harassed a tall, stately blue heron, trying to hunt for frogs by the shore. The ducks swam into his space, causing him to take flight with his enormous wings. He landed just a few meters away, so the ducks quickly swam into his space again, forcing him back to his first spot. What an entertaining sight.

Back at the cabin, we had just enough time to clean up. After moving all our gear to the cars, we found a picnic table up on a little hill with a good view of the dock, so we could play just a few more games and watch the new campers loading up their canoes for their adventures into God's breathtaking beauty.

The easy lunch tasted good in the shade. We took turns saying grace before our meals, giving thanks for God's care and the evidence of all His blessings, love, and incredible creativity. I felt especially thankful that even though we had canoed for maybe two hours the first day, more the second day, hiked for two hours, and then paddled again today for over an hour, no one had any sore muscles. We are tough, strong ladies.

We had been blessed with perfect weather, had fun canoeing in the clear waters of Algonquin Park amidst gorgeous scenery, and walked in the rejuvenating wilderness with the cozy company of caring new friends. We hated to have our time here come to an end. Good times fly by far too fast.

Thank you, Rain Lake and Algonquin Park, for the wonderful memories.

Thank you, ladies, for your fun friendship.

Bear in the Area

Mew Lake

How many times can I drag my husband into the backcountry wilderness of Algonquin Park? Doug is a computer geek, addicted to TV and all his techy gadgets. These would not work even if he could bring it all in the canoe and over all the portages. So, I must compromise and see who else I can talk into coming with me, one way or another, to spare my caring, giving husband some hardships. Just some.

My Judo buddy, Linda, eagerly said she would come again. We found two other willing ladies to join us. Oh, I know that they don't want anything too rough or wild.

- How close to nature do they want to get?
- Canoe trip into the wilderness in tiny tents? Noooooo.
- Bigger tents in bigger, busier campgrounds? No, maybe not a tent.
- Well then, a lodge? Too expensive.
- Another old Ranger's cabin? Most of these are only accessible by canoe.

- OK then, I know. A yurt!

Look at that! They said yes. Hooray. I explained what a yurt is, and they agreed it would be good. What is a yurt? Well, not a cabin and not a tent but a good compromise with a hard floor, real roof and thick canvas walls. These come equipped with electric lights, heaters, a small table with

31

six chairs, and two bunk beds, the bottom bunk being a double bed. Outside is a wooden roof over a BBQ, a picnic table, and a fire pit.

One hesitant lady asked, "What about bears?" Of course, I reassured her that I had never seen a bear in any camping area in Algonquin Park, either in the main campgrounds or the interior, on all the many, many occasions that I had been camping.

So, in March (the needed five-month advance time), I reserved a yurt right on the shores of Mew Lake, just off the main road through Algonquin Park. Three nights and four days in early September.

I impatiently waited until summer arrived before I began bugging them with more details about our trip. I could only hope they felt as excited as I did. Maybe my enthusiasm inspired them as I sent countless pictures of our previous camping adventure, other pictures of Algonquin Park, and information on all the things to see and do: museum, art gallery, visitor's centre, outdoor theatre, gift stores, and restaurants, hiking trails, canoe rental, beaches to sunbathe on and lakes to swim in.

Finally, the day arrived. The ladies from Kitchener would arrive at Algonquin Park close to noon, and we met at our yurt campsite.

Oh dear. This sign greeted them:

So, my priority was to hand everyone a whistle to wear at all times while outside. Thankfully, we never had a chance to actually use them.

What a fun reunion. What a delightful abode. We picked out our bunks and found the water tap, the outhouse, and the path to the comfort station. Then we walked to the beach. But too soon, a soft rain began. So, we headed back inside to play games and indulge in many snacks.

The roofed shelter of the BBQ kept me dry while I made supper in the drizzle. When the rain stopped, we made a fire and enjoyed the bug-free evening, cozy and peaceful, in our private campsite with warm friends, right on the shore of Mew Lake.

Excitement for our next day's adventures made falling asleep a little elusive. But the thought of the chilly walk to the outhouse kept us snuggled in our sleeping bags until the early morning light. Well, most of us. I love a walk in the dark, so if I must get out of my warm bed, I don't mind too much. No flashlight is needed until I close the door to the tiny outhouse. Now acclimatized to the chill of the night, I can enjoy a slow walk back while I study the stars and try to determine what time it is.

*

Soon enough, the morning dawned bright and warm. How did we get to eat breakfast with all the chatter of planning our day? With so much that Algonquin has to offer, what shall we take in first?

I pulled out my treasured and torn map and the annual Algonquin newspaper to show the ladies where and what our options were. Some attractions we could save for a rainy day, like the museum, art gallery, and Visitor's Centre. Today the sun shone warm in a clear sky.

The priority would be to paddle Canoe Lake, which meant I could impress them with the story of Tom Thomson. Since I have heard Doug tell the tale a multitude of times, ad nauseum, I could now also be considered an expert on every single detail. But I stuck to the highlights.

After our coffee, we cleaned up. With the possibility of a bear in the area, dirty dishwater must be dumped down the outhouse hole. Before we headed to Canoe Lake, all food, dishes, cleaning supplies and even toiletries must be cleaned up and packed into the car.

We rented two canoes and paddled past the spot where Tom's body had been found and then on to the north end of the lake. These ladies are not accustomed to paddling for an hour against a bit of wind. It felt good to pull our canoes up on the rocky shore and rest our arms. Here our legs had a good workout, climbing up the steep rocks to the totem and memorial to a canoeist, wilderness guide and a great artist who inspired all Canadians with his paintings of Algonquin Park's beauty.

Lunch at the top gave us a good view of most of the lake, and I could tell more of Tom's story. Everyone loves story time.

As Frank Braucht said,

"With canoe, paddle and packsack,
He wandered far afield,
Searching the Master's gallery
For treasures it might yield.

The mystery of his tragic death,
Was sealed within this man;
Yet may his life inspire us all,
A life so brief in span."

Once off the lake, we headed down the road to Tea Lake Dam. Such beauty and power of the racing river. Since we still had energy, we climbed up and up the Hardwood Lookout trail. The spectacular view makes hiking over rocks and roots very worthwhile.

*

The next day dawned clear and bright, allowing us to do lots more hiking. With so many trails to choose from, picking one could be difficult. We had two shorter ones within walking distance of the Mew Lake campground. These took us to fantastic lookout points viewing the green expanse of trees and lakes. Wow.

So far, no bears!

We drove to the Opeongo canoe rental and paddled leisurely down
Costello Creek. When it appeared, we could go no further as the creek
narrowed and bulrushes and tall grasses crowded in; we found a smooth,
sun-warmed rock to have lunch on. Then we meandered back up to the
Opeongo store and sat at the picnic table to wonder at the vast size of Lake
Opeongo. The store, with all its souvenirs, greatly entertained the ladies as
well.

After all the walking, we had to swim and lay on the warm sandy
beach. After all the fresh, clean air, bright sun, and lots of good exercise,
we surely slept well.

*

On our last morning, we had to clean up our campsite. Having to leave
is the worst part of camping. But we still had to do just one more hike.

Finally, a very leisurely stroll through the gift store at Canoe Lake. Lunch is always entertaining by the restaurant's windows at Canoe Lake, watching campers head out in their canoes. Fun times. Good memories. Lots of pictures to share. Happy friends. And thankfully, no bears!

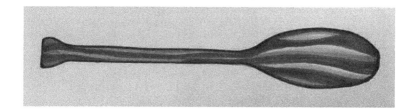

Plan B

Tea Lake

I finally planned my first venture into canoe camping. Our two daughters eagerly agreed to come. So, I called Algonquin Park to reserve our route two weeks in advance.

But. Don't you hate "buts"?

Did you know that wilderness camping is so popular, especially from the access point at Canoe Lake, that it is advisable to book your trip as early as five months in advance? I was too late. We could not take my long-hoped for wilderness canoe trip this time.

First lesson: Book your canoe trips five months in advance.

Second lesson: Always have a plan B.

We took our little trailer, much to Doug's pleasure. But it does not sleep four, so we three ladies slept in the trailer, and since Doug snores, he had to sleep in a tiny tent anyway. The small Tea Lake campground has a lovely beach and easy access for day trip exploring.

Doug is obsessed with Canadian artist Tom Thomson and his murder mystery, so on our first day, we paddled the entire Canoe Lake to show our daughters all the historic sites.

The store at the bottom of Canoe Lake provides a map of these points of interest, so it began. We found the spot where Tom's canoe had been found and, further on, where his body appeared. We paddled past the cottage of his girlfriend and the cottage of his enemy, implicated in his demise.

Near the top end of the lake, we sat on a smooth rocky shore to have lunch before trekking through the forest to find the remains of the Mowat Lodge, where Tom had stayed. Then we hiked down a dirt trail, avoided a large pile of bear scat, through a swamp and, up a hill, through thick forest until we finally found the presumed location of his gravesite.

Paddling further up the lake, we wandered up Potter's Creek to discover where the old town of Canoe Lake had been. Almost nothing remains to indicate how busy it had been one hundred years ago. Back in the days when the train allowed the only access into Algonquin Park, a town grew, with a hospital, school, and big hotel had about two hundred residents and many summer tourists.

J.R. Booth's logging camps employed many, within the park. Pictures from that time show only a few sparse trees in this area. Hard to believe all this history with so little evidence remaining of that busy spot.

Returning to the lake, we found Tom's memorial on the north shore. It is a short but very steep climb to the amazing lookout. A large stone memorial and tall totem pole tell some of his life. Hidden at the back of the totem is an inspired poem.

We jumped in our canoes and headed back to our campsite. The sisters had a head start. I thought Doug and I were in good shape, but no matter how hard we tried, we could not catch up to those slim, trim girls. What a good day of paddling and exploring.

*

We took it easier on our second day, but still we discovered much beauty. Leaving the beach at our campground, we leisurely followed

Smoke Creek and headed south, this time to Smoke Lake. We slowed to find pretty water lilies in the shallow bays. Beauty hiding everywhere surprised us. We passed a few rocky points and viewed many rustic cottages before returning to our campground for a swim.

Lots of exercise, fresh air, warm sun, sparkling water, and beautiful views filled our short two days.

I am so thankful for the memorable time with our girls. I am so grateful to God for this fun bonding time with our cherished daughters.

Wolves!
Basin Lake

You may want to try an easy, short introduction to wilderness canoe camping without the work of paddling for days with back-bending portages. I have the solution. I thought this idea would ease Doug into wilderness camping and maybe teach me how to do it.

With the canoe and gear loaded up, we drove to a pretty little lake on the southeast side of Algonquin Park. The slow winding picturesque drive up Turners Road along the Little Bonnechere River has a few hiking trails hidden in the forests.

The narrow dirt road walled with forest opens up at the Basin Lake Depot cabin. This is now the oldest building in all of Algonquin Park. One hundred years ago, the few farming settlements here serviced three logging camps, hid even further back in the wilderness. At different times, this cabin served as a school, a hospital, an office for the logging camps and then an Algonquin Park Ranger's cabin. Not far from this cabin are two gravesites, one for men who died at the logging camps and the other for the farmers' children who died of diphtheria.

We could have parked by the old cabin and carried everything down the fairly level ATV trail to Basin Lake, but we chose to drive as branches swept the dirt off the sides of our little car.

Basin Lake has only a very few campsites. You must camp at a marked campsite, which has a level spot for a tent or two, and a fire pit which may be surrounded by a log bench. Some campsites have a counter that some creative camper has constructed out of branches and rope, between two trees. Of course, you are wondering now about another necessary item. You must hunt for the tiny trail into the forest to the thunderbox. Yes, it is just a box with a hinged lid that, when lifted, reveals a hole. Ta, da! Your washroom facility.

Do **not** forget to pack toilet paper.

We found the best campsite on an island at the top end of the lake. What a panoramic view.

We had warm weather, a clear sky, singing birds and laughing loons. After I swam around the island, we sat in joyful wonder, watching a mama and baby beaver playing across the narrow waterway between us and the lake's reedy north shore.

Darkness softly covered us to display a spectacular, sparkly sky. Doug, the astronomer, easily pointed out constellations.

Soon enough, I realized that I had forgotten to bring a flashlight. The tiny path to the thunderbox is hard enough to find in the daylight, and I discovered that getting lost or disoriented in the darkness is quite easy. With the help of Doug's snoring and a full moon, I managed to find my way back to our tiny tent.

Do **not** forget to pack a flashlight.

Sleep came easy in my cozy warm sleeping bag. A lone, long, mystical wolf howl over the nearby hills woke me. Not long after, mama wolf's musical response came from an opposing direction which seemed so close. Soon a party erupted as many puppies practiced their howls in a joyful racket. What fun! How blessed I felt to be able to hear these elusive wolves.

*

The bright, warming morning sun came too soon. After a leisurely breakfast over a small fire, I hunted the entire island in search of the tiny birds that lived there. What beauty. What peace.

Later came the inevitable packing up and the return home. Surely a trip too short. Too short but long enough to fill me with a greater passion for longer canoe trips deeper into God's wonderful nature.

I will never forget the wolves.

Cut Short

Rain Lake to Sawyer Lake

Anticipation obliterated any possibility of sleep the night before our trip. I paced in the dark. I contemplated everything I had packed, hoping that I had remembered everything. Had I packed too much, making our portages too strenuous?

I learned some lessons. This time I would get it right.

Plan far ahead. Done.

Reserve campsites. Done.

Rent canoes. Done.

Pick a short easy route to ease us into canoe camping. Done.

Doug and I, our older daughter and a friend, would start at Rain Lake, portage to spend the first night on Sawyer Lake, the second night on Jubilee Lake, and return to spend the third night on Rain Lake.

Plan, prepare and pack meals. Done.

Pack all the gear and repack. Done.

Wandering in our dark apartment, mere hours before departure time, my foot slammed into a solid wooden chair leg. I knew immediately that two toes had broken. I struggled to remain quiet while I sat on the couch, pushed the toes back into place, and wrapped them in ice. I know broken toes and how to wrap injuries from experience. What horrible timing. But determination forced me to hide my pain and keep it a secret from Doug and the girls. Anticipation and desire kept me going.

In the early morning, we packed everything into the car, picked up our daughter and a friend, and headed north from our southern Ontario home. I refused to limp or give any indication of the nasty pain I felt. Nothing would detour this trip. Just before we reached Algonquin Park's office in Kearney, north of Huntsville, I quietly confessed to Doug what I had done.

"What? How can you manage a canoe trip? How can you do the portages?"

"Shhh. No one has to know. I have them wrapped and held snuggly in my shoe. Canoeing is sitting and easy. Our only portage today, to Sawyer Lake, is not long. By tomorrow they should be better able to handle the portage to our next campsite on Jubilee Lake."

We picked up our permits and drove down the road to the canoe rental store to pick up the paddles and life jackets. Our canoes waited for us at Rain Lake.

My excitement mounted as we drove down the road, which soon lost its pavement and grew steadily narrower until it resembled an ATV trail. We all wondered if we were lost even though signs assured us that Rain Lake lay ahead. Other signs warned us to beware of logging trucks. What? On this tiny path? How would we ever avoid a huge truck and the tree branches reaching for us?

Suddenly the sun flooded us as we emerged from the cover of the trees to a large parking area packed tight with possibly one hundred cars and pick-up trucks. But not a human in sight. Everyone had gone for days or weeks into the interior of Algonquin Park. My dream. In a few minutes, we headed off too. But not before Doug had fallen into the water. We all laughed long and loud. Poor dear.

What a perfect day with sunny, warm weather. Except for the throbbing pain in my foot.

Passing grassy bays along this narrow end of the lake, a pair of black ducks hurried to hide in the bulrushes. Soon the lake opened up to a pretty view and a large island right ahead. But dark clouds approached us. As we neared the end of the lake, thunder threatened.

We got over the easy portage with all our gear and canoes before the lightning and rain began. We pulled out our rain gear, huddled under our tarp, and watched other paddlers arrive. Rain flooded down the path beside us.

Totally shocked, we watched some canoeists jump in their canoes and take off down the lake amidst the deafening thunder and flashing lightning. They explained that they had far to go to keep to their planned route. "We will hug the shoreline, and we will be fine."

No way could we believe that. So, we waited under our tarp and prayed for their safety.

Finally, after two hours, the storm dwindled to a drizzle. We jumped back into our canoes and headed down Sawyer Lake to find a vacant campsite.

Doug set up the tents while I unpacked the little propane stove to make our lunch and coffee. The girls hunted for firewood that we hoped might not be too waterlogged. We needed the campfire to dry Doug's soggy shoes. Would they ever dry in this damp, on and off again drizzle?

We found the thunderbox at the end of a long, winding, narrow path up the hill. A couple of big piles of moose scat made the walk tricky.

We all so enjoyed being in the wilderness, with no sight of humans or traffic sounds. The girls explored our campsite and named a visiting loon, Philip. He entertained us with his preening, summersaults, and diving.

The total darkness brought sleep easily to everyone, cozy in our warm, dry sleeping bags. Everyone except me. My entire foot throbbed. The multiple trips up the hill to the thunderbox intensified my agony.

*

By morning's light, I could see that my entire foot had turned a nasty, dark blue. I wondered if I had also broken one of my foot's tiny bones. What had I done? Of course, I had only aggravated my foot and given it no time to heal. Doug thought I should have a doctor look at it.

The dark skies warned us of more rain and chilling temperatures coming. Even though I had warned the girls to bring warm clothes and good running shoes, our young friend only had short shorts and flip-flops.

Too many negatives cut our trip short, and the disappointment wounded me more than the toes.

We packed up, and Doug could finally put on dry shoes. As he flipped the canoes to bring them back down to the water, one canoe quickly escaped his grasp and slid into the lake. Doug ran down the slope, jumped into the water, and captured the runaway canoe. Poor dear. Now he had to wear soggy shoes for another day.

We enjoyed our paddle back, taking our time to appreciate the contrasting sizes, shapes, and colours of the various trees lining the lakes. Rocks edged some of the shoreline, a few grassy bays almost concealed a Great Blue Heron, and on a rocky island, the old ruins of a large stone fireplace made us wonder what stories it held.

We spent the rest of the day in Huntsville. Doug and I sat too long at the hospital waiting, waiting, only to learn that my two toes were indeed broken, but the rest of my foot remained intact. The doctor assured me that no medical intervention would be needed and that my wrapping job would be fine enough for my toes.

The two girls entertained themselves, touring this busy tourist town's fun little gift stores. We returned home, and Doug could finally dry his feet and shoes. My toes could rest and recuperate. But the pain of my disappointment remained.

The two girls never stopped smiling during our entire adventure and promised they would love to come another time for a more extended trip, as long as I promised not to break any more toes.

No Silence in the Night

Grand Lake. Written from Doug's point of view.

Well, my wife finally convinced me to go on a two-night canoe trip. We have this cozy and comfortable little pop-up trailer to go camping with. I love that thing. But now Liz has this crazy obsession with canoe trips. I can't call it a midlife crisis unless she lives to be one hundred and thirty. She just might, though. I can't even call it menopause madness. Hopefully, she is outgrown that. Hopefully.

Maybe she should be a saleswoman. She knew just how to sell the idea of canoe camping on Grand Lake. I am a fan of history and Tom Thomson, who spent time on this lake. One hundred years ago, the tiny town of Achray stood on the shores of Grand Lake. The old Canadian Northern Railway line that William MacKenzie and Donald Mann completed building in 1915 ran from Ottawa to Sudbury and passed through here. The railways and lumber industries within the Algonquin Park area helped establish many small settlements along the rail line. The names and locations can be found on Algonquin Park's canoe routes map. It would be quite the adventure to hunt for what might remain of these communities hidden in the dense forest.

At the far southeast corner of Algonquin Park, the long, winding, dusty gravel Achray Road (or Barron Canyon Road) brings you past a popular trail to the three-hundred-foot cliffs of the Barron Gorge. Spectacular views. Jagged cliffs drop straight down to the dark one-hundred-foot depths of the river. You may peer over the edge to see some canoes drifting along like tiny bugs. So many good look-out spots. Please don't go too close. I have a fear and a fascination with heights.

Travel further down the road brings you to the Achray campgrounds and jump-off point for a couple of canoe routes. One route heads south and takes you along the base of these tall red cliffs. Years ago, we paddled here with our kids for a day trip accessing the river from the southern end.

At the campground on Grand Lake is a small old cabin with informative plaques of Tom Thomson's time in the area. A short trail takes you to a plaque near the very spot where Tom painted the famous *Jack Pine*.

60

Since Tom spent time here, I guess I would have to camp on this lake too. The campground has many large, private sites for tents, trailers, and RVs right along the shore and a big, beautiful beach area as well. But we loaded our canoe, and instead of heading south towards the multiple portages to the canyon, we headed north on this long lake to explore. No portaging for us this time. Although I am apprehensive as to what Liz is planning for the future.

What about our little high and dry and comfortable trailer? Nope. Now I have to go back to sleeping in a tent. Oh, my aching back.

After we explored a good part of the long narrow lake, we found a nice site with a large flat area covered in fragrant reddish pine needles. Now where to put the tent and tarp? How can that be hard? How can that cause so much discussion? Discussion is a nice word for it.

Liz discovered that when she had hugged a pine tree while tying up a tarp rope, the end of her braid had come into contact with a huge glob of pine gum. What a disgusting sticky mess, as though her hair was glued together. We had nothing that would wash it out. Impossible to remove. But she quickly came up with a temporary fix before I could suggest that we return home to get her cleaned up.

She rammed her sticky braid into a sock and fastened it securely. Not so pretty, but for now, it would do, she said. I guess it's okay if she looks a little wild in the wilderness.

But with such a beautiful view and a warm, bright day, our moods quickly returned to sunny.

61

This summer had been very sunny with no rain most of July, causing a total fire ban in the area. We rarely have a campfire. No loss there. And we had a tiny propane one-burner stove for cooking. We found a big pine branch and swept all the pine needles away from the fire pit area where we would place the stove and cook. By we, I mean Liz. You do not want me near any kind of stove.

That night rain fell. Of course. No rain for a month but when we go camping in a tent, it rains.

*

Morning brought bright warm sun again, so we packed up and headed out to hunt for another campsite.

We enjoyed a leisurely paddle on the shiny, calm waters. Soon enough, we found our home for this night. A huge smooth rocky point and a good flat spot for a tent. And a fantastic view.

We got all set up and watched campers on the far shores. Liz went swimming, long and far, alone. No way do I swim.

Now she had a soggy sticky braid. But she said she could not put up with it any longer. So, are we going home then?

Nope, not a chance. She had another solution of sorts. We had brought a big, dangerous-looking knife. She asked me to cut off the sticky end of her braid. What? Me cut hair? But this extremely dull knife could only cut butter. She laid her head down on the log bench and stretched out her goopy lump of hair. I had to saw it off with a lot of pressure and fuss and bother. With the nasty deed finally done, she could finally comb her hair. Miraculously it didn't look too bad.

After that bit of excitement, I watched other campers, paddlers, and swimmers. Did I mention that Liz packed us no chairs? She assured me that sitting on a life jacket against a tree would work just fine. So now what? We just sit here, then? Did you know that life jackets slide on pine needles turning your sitting into slouching, into laying? Bored now.

But I guess I do have to admit that it was a great view, perfect weather, and tasty food. I can survive without my computer for one day, but maybe not without a chair. Oh, my aching back.

Enough sitting. We had a tall hill behind us, so we hiked easily to the summit on a primarily smooth rock trail. Now there was a fantastic view. That's what I'm talking about.

Sleep comes easily to me. But not that night. Okay, it was fun listening to the bull frogs' bass choir. When they concluded, the loons continued the concert. A very typical Algonquin experience.

But then, on the branch directly above our tent, a whip-or-will began. When I say "began," one would assume there is an ending. But whip-or-wills never stop. Never. They don't even pause to take a breath. So loud. So long. So annoying. Well, I guess Liz didn't find them annoying since she kept giggling at my grumbling.

Somehow, I fell asleep. But not long after, a terrifying thunderous noise woke me and caused such panic that I would have bolted right through that tent wall if Liz had not captured me. Surely the hill behind us must have exploded.

But no. Liz, never fearful Liz, calmed me and explained that the dreadful rumble came from a low-flying huge Hercules plane from the Armed Forces Base in nearby Petawawa doing training exercises above us, so low that you could almost count the rivets in the fuselage. What a fright. How could I go back to sleep after that craziness? Somehow peace, silence, and sleep returned.

The next morning shone bright and beautiful again for our leisurely paddle and the return drive home.

I do have to admit that I absolutely do feel the wonder of the peaceful beauty that must have captivated Tom. I feel the peace that must draw us closer to the Creator.

I wonder where Liz will want to go next. What will be our next adventure? Will I ever be able to sleep in my comfy trailer and bring my laptop and comfortable large camp chair again?

Thunder Box? That's a problem.

Lake Magnetawan to Little Trout Lake

Written from the point of view of Chris Border, my daughter's partner.

OK, so I willingly agreed to go on a canoe trip into the wilderness of Algonquin Park with April. No problem there. And with her parents, who seem to be pretty nice. I don't know what it will be like to live with them for four days, though. Just her parents. Isolated...... It should be doable.

But they are a little religious, and with no distractions like cell phone, TV, computer, or email, what if they take this captive audience opportunity to preach? How would that be? That might be a problem.

Then I was warned that I'd have to wear a bear whistle at all times. That is a little concerning. Would bears be a problem?

But what really made me question my decision came with the information about the thunderbox. I had to ask about the washroom facilities, didn't I? Just a box out in the open with no protection from wild weather and all animals, although adorable. And no privacy? I don't know if I'm liking this. That **is** a problem.

I'm not even all that athletic like April, who is almost obsessed with working out. But I guess if her parents, who must be twice my age think they can do this, then who am I to miss an opportunity to be in the beautiful wilderness of Algonquin Park in a tiny tent with my gorgeous babe?

So we made plans, and the date drew near. The constant texting between my girlfriend and her Mom let me know how excited she felt: what to bring, how to pack, who would supply what, when and where to meet and who knows what else they talked about. Until now, we had been camping in campgrounds close to our southern Ontario home. This is our first adventure, far from home, canoeing into the wilderness.

April had wanted to do this kind of trip for so long, and many previous trips had been messed up due to the injury and illness of others. I could see how much this meant to her, so I had to help with this long-time desire. A guy has to understand his babe's desires, right?

Well, we were up and on the road way too early. I'm surprised she even let me drive. We made it to our rendezvous more than half an hour ahead of schedule. We grabbed a quick snack at Timmy's and took off for, where now? North of Huntsville? After getting our permit and instructions to find the rented canoes, we headed off toward the lake. The pavement ended. The road got smaller and smaller, dusty and snaky. The trees crowded ever closer, which almost caused me some claustrophobia. Is this even a road any more or an ATV trail? Tight curves on gravel are nasty for a city driver. Would it never end? Would my dope, brand-new shiny black car survive this torture? Are we even in Ontario anymore? We must be lost.

April just kept giggling at my grunts and gasps and sighs. On the rare occasion that I took my eyes off this narrow, very curvy path, I caught a glimpse of the wonderful wilderness. So much to see, tiny streams, clear rivers, flowered swamps, shiny ponds, beaver dams, beaver lodges, steep rocky cliffs, and a tall tree growing right out of the top of a huge bolder. Amazing beauty. So, this is why we are doing this. Maybe I should giggle too.

Finally, we arrived at a massive parking lot. There had to be one hundred cars crammed into that clearing. No people…oh wait, there are three people here. With all these cars, you would expect to hear the noise of many people. But the silence surprised me and allowed me the needed calm after that punishing path. Stepping out of the car into the warm sunshine, I breathed deeply to get rid of the dust from the last forty-five minutes and to drink in the wonderfully refreshing pure air. Clean, unpolluted air made me want to keep breathing slowly and deeply. The sweet aroma of cedar and pine sparked excitement for this trip.

I heard the intricate strange new song of a bird. But I couldn't find him in the multitude of branches above us.

A short walk through the forest took us to the lake, erasing the bad taste of the city smog and dusty drive. Wow. Wilderness. No houses. No people. Green trees, blue sky, and clear water of the aqua lake caused everyone to smile, for sure.

We loaded up and took off, full of energy, over Lake Magnetawan to the first portage. So this is what a portage is. Off with the shoes and step into the water. Pull the canoe onto shore and offload our packs. On with the shoes, carry our gear over rocks and roots to Hambone Lake. Then back over the path to get the canoes. April's Mom assured me that April had carried the canoe solo. What? I have never had to carry a canoe. How do we coordinate this? Somehow, we made it.

Across Hambone Lake and the next portage, we arrived at the much bigger Ralph Bice Lake. Wow, again. Such a spectacular view. But the sky is not so blue anymore. Clouds closed in. Halfway down this large lake, we found a scenic campsite. After the work of paddling and portaging for three hours, this picturesque spot is so worth the work. We explored, selected a spot for our tent, and collected wood for the fire pit, which somehow sparked exhilaration. A rejuvenating change from the daily city routine.

April's Mom anticipated our craving for coffee and lunch. Yum.

With a group struggle, we managed to tie up the big tarp before the rain arrived. And by big, I mean ridiculously massive.

But where is the thunder box? Where? I had to follow a tiny path through the bush, up a hill, and over rocks and roots. Ah. There it sat. It was just as they said, private and secluded, open and exposed to the elements, like rain.

The rain began.

We ran for the cover of the tarp and a fun game of cards. Sitting on the ground became a problem as streams trickled down the hill and under us.

Oh, the joy of camping.

"Seriously, does it have to rain every time we go camping? If so, I'm going to have to rethink this."

"I know exactly how you feel," April's Dad quickly responded.

"For sure, but I still love camping. It's still good. We brought raincoats." added Mom.

With a bit of rearranging, we kept dry. The slow, gentle rain cleaned out the city stress from my brain. It stopped before dark, in time to take in our view of the large lake and phantom island shrouded in mist. We took turns with binoculars to study the lake for other paddlers.

Time for a campfire. Guys, and even girls evidently, like to play with fire. April had too much fun with the fire.

The rich, musty scent of the soggy leaves and pine needles and the musical loons felt therapeutic after the day's hard work.

Man, I really wanted to see a moose. Piles of moose turds along the path near the shore made me wonder, "Where are the moose?"

April and Dad washed the dishes. Then Dad showed me how he makes drinking water. An ultraviolet wand sterilizes lots of filtered drinking water in just a couple of minutes. What a fun toy. He had to share that job with me.

One major chore must be done before the sun sets. Mom hunted for a branch to hang the food bag. It must be very high, big enough to hold the weight of our food, and far enough away from any tree trunk or other branches to be inaccessible to critters. Not so easy to find the right spot. I managed to throw the rope over said branch, which I discovered could be a dangerous task. Having attached the rope to a rock, I catapulted the rope over the branch. But what goes up must come down. We had to run for cover! We almost got whacked. The rock went up and finally, after multiple attempts, made it over the right branch. Success. The bag hung high in the growing twilight.

*

Early to bed, early to rise. Mom must have been up with the sun as she showed us the awesome picture she captured as she served the coffee and breakfast.

The calm water mirrored the bright sun.

Then we were up and out-a there. In the loaded canoes, we paddled until the lake narrowed and looped around rocks and a peninsula to the far end. Where is the end? Where is the portage? How can anyone figure out where that tiny yellow sign is amid all this green shoreline? Impossible. Oh good, magically, another canoe appeared on the lake ahead of us. I guess we are headed in the right direction. Honestly, I had doubts as to how April's parents could ever know where to go.

Wack. This portage was nowhere near as short or smooth as the two from yesterday. What hard work. But April bolted out of the canoe as though spring-loaded and raced over all the rocks, roots, hills, and mud holes as if she had helium in those big backpacks. What's up with that?

The warm sunshine invigorated me. The challenge motivated me. The adventure is addictive. There was no way I wanted her to get far ahead of me. I stuck right with her. But that Dad of hers followed tight on my heels. How could this old dude possibly move so quickly, all loaded up with too many packs? At least her Mom had the sense to take it easy.

We paddled along this new lake and passed large islands and rocks sticking out of the middle of the open expanse. How's that happen?

Then the hunt began for our second campsite. We passed many good spots that were already occupied. All, of course, are so secluded that you have the illusion of being alone on the lake. Not alone. Gulls called. Loons sang. They really do sing and laugh. Six loons chatted it up.

We finally found what we hoped to be the perfect campsite. Okay, I felt tired of paddling, but it did look like a good one. First, we had to check it out, at least. Mom looked for level spots for the tents. Dad looked for trees to hang the tarp. April hunted for firewood for this super fire pit surrounded by a comfy log bench, as comfortable as logs can be at least. My immediate task was to look for the thunderbox.

No. No. Now we have a problem. This site would not do. No way. Look. From where the tents would sit, you could clearly see the thunderbox. No way did I want to stay here. Nope. This was wack.

I guess. Mom was even more tired from paddling than me because she came up with a fresh solution. The clear sky and the favourable forecast said no rain so the tarp could be used as a wall. Let me at 'er. I made that sucker into the best obstruction ever seen in these parts. No problem.

With lunch made, the tents up, the wood collected, a suitable tree for the food bag selected, and the thunderbox, hidden behind the massive blue wall of privacy, we could drink all the coffee and eat all the beans we desired without hesitation or apprehension.

We had lots of time to enjoy this wonderful fresh wilderness. But April claimed that she wanted to stay here. I mean, to **stay** here, live here, remain here in the wilderness, and never return to civilization. I had a problem with that. But I had to keep quiet for now.

We took a short excursion to the end of the lake just to hike the next portage and be able to say that we had made it to Little Queer Lake.

The day was dope, the water warm and inviting. Or maybe it's those noisy loons that invited us in for a swim. But I do not swim. April and her Mom are fish. No. Oops, my bad. Mom explains that they are not fish but mermaids. Which would make me a flotation device as I had to wear a life jacket to join them in their swim out to a tiny rock island. Loons to the right and loons to the left serenaded us in stereo. Or maybe they just laughed at the kicking and splashing I tried to pass off as swimming. April and Mom made it out to the center of the lake effortlessly. I felt exhausted. But I laughed.

We loved the sun-baked rocky shore that warmed us up after the chilly, fresh, clean waters. Fun with my babe in a bathing suit. Dope.

Somehow investigating the opposite shoreline with binoculars kept April and Dad entertained. Paddlers waved and spoke briefly as they passed by in their search for their next campsite.

A huge, massive, even, metallic black beetle came to visit. I had to get that camera. It crawled slowly across the bolder that doubled as our table. He gave us ample time to admire his handsomeness. Then Junior willingly climbed onto a little stick so we could study his acrobatics. Better than the nature channel.

"So where's the big wildlife?" I wanted to know.

"Chris is so hoping to see a moose," April explains.

Mom pointed and said, "Take a careful stroll down that path. They have definitely been here often".

Exploring our area showed evidence of these enormous creatures. I've been told they are large, but I've never seen one. These giant piles of droppings indicate that moose must be massive. I had to watch my step, for sure. Man, I'd love to see a moose.

Supper time. I definitely enjoyed that good, big vegan meal and the big blazing campfire. So quiet. So calm. So beautiful. I could almost agree with April's desire just to stay here forever. Maybe without her parents. But Mom seemed to want to make this home too.

"Hey, Dad, tell Chris about Tom Thomson." Someone else from the city who fell in love with Algonquin Park and had to capture it in his awe-inspiring paintings. Dad told us every detail he could remember from the many books he had read about the murder mystery of young, talented Tom.

Stars came out. So dark. What a big endless universe. Gives a man reason to contemplate eternity and broadens horizons and possibilities. Gives life a different, bigger, better perspective.

Mom pointed out the star Vega and said, "That is where we really came from since we are Vegans." Hilarious. Yawn.

Then another life form arrived. Torturous tiny vampires. Not enough dragonflies in the night to ward off the mosquitoes. Good reason to retreat to our tents. Oh well. Not as wack as rain forcing us to run for cover.

Loons' magical calls lulled us to sleep. Night all.

*

Morning softly arrived, warm and bright, promising another perfect day. Fresh.

I felt full of energy with only a bit of sore muscles. We packed up after breakfast and headed back to Ralph Bice Lake. This longer portage seemed even longer going this way. It must be mostly uphill and had way too many rocks and roots, as was proven by the ones that grabbed Dad and broke his toe. Ouch. Poor guy. How could he carry that heavy pack and then the canoe with a broken toe?

Crossing this end of Ralph Bice Lake made me think I should have paid more attention coming this way the first time so I'd have some clue which way to head going back. Somehow Mom seemed to know. That's our reason for staying a bit behind them. Not so they couldn't see me wince in pain because of all my sore muscles. Oh no. Not at all.

At this narrow end of the lake, we travelled close to shore. Watching the rocks and shrubs zip by, it felt like we had a good speed. As the lake grew larger and we wandered further from shore, the immensity and distances made this man feel small and slow.

Even though our two canoes started off together and we tried to stay close, somehow, we drifted apart.

The hot sun baked us from a blue, blue sky. Can't get this spectacular colour in the city. Can't get this freshness, this pure beauty in the city. Water so clear you can see twenty feet down. Green trees surrounded us on all the shorelines. I could see no one else. No campsites, no other canoes. We could be hundreds of miles from anyone right there.

Makes a person want to do some imagining. Makes a person want to sit here for a while in the middle of this expanse of open water enveloped by the opposite of man's chaos. What if this were a different time in history? What if man hadn't polluted, paved, and poisoned so much of the earth? What if it could all be still, calm, clean, and pristine? What if we could live in friendship with all the wild creatures?

Oh man. Too much dreaming. April's an excellent paddler, even steering in the stern. I hoped she didn't notice that my contemplation caused a pause in my stride......just for a second, or...

The wind picked up. Against us, of course. Now I had to give 'er. Pour it on. Ouch. Then I really noticed those sore muscles.

April's parents headed closer to shore. They tried to tell us something, but the wind snatched it before we could catch it. I finally understood that all their pointing meant they were looking for our next campsite.

We paddled harder against the wind and the growing waves. Faster. Deeper strokes. See? Doesn't paddling sound like fun? Not. Not with sore arms. Arms that silently begged us to find a campsite soon.

This spot looked good. Yes? No? Maybe? April and I checked out a high spot and her parents went ahead to check out the next lower one. Good thing our cell phones worked. Amazing. With some quick scoring, our campsite earned a six, but theirs got a seven. With the vote in their favour, we headed to our last camp across the bay.

After some exploration, we all agreed that this site must really be an eight, at least. Good view, level tent sites, a big fire pit, lots of wood, even a choice of trees for the food bag, and **most** important of all, the well-secluded thunderbox was pretty close on a fairly level path. No wall needed. No problem at all.

But I still hadn't seen a moose, even though we found lots more evidence here as well.

Mom got the coffee and lunch on, April collected wood, Dad and I put the tents up, and I even secured a rope in a good tree for the food bag. We had a good routine now. I realized this would be our last night of this almost dreaded trip. This greatly enjoyed trip. This perfect trip with perfect weather and perfect campsites. Wow. Made me wish it would last longer. Made me almost agree with April and want just to stay here and not return to the stinking, noisy city. Made me determine that another wilderness canoe camping trip is doable. Definitely. No problem.

So we sat and enjoyed the view. This was the widest part of this long lake. The longer, narrower part that we had just traversed was blocked from our view by a large island. The green of the forest touched the entire shore except directly across from us. On the far side we could see an area of tall sheer rock cliffs. It must reach a height of one hundred feet. Maybe we need to stay another day to climb and explore.

Mom slid off the smooth rocky shoreline for a swim. Dad dug out the binoculars and began to look bored. Mom told us that he was, by now, going through withdrawal from his computer and TV.

A surprise visitor drifted up to spend some time with us. Such a relaxed and even peaceful fellow. His cheery smile hid the strength he undoubtedly possessed. His slow approach contradicted his infamous reputation. Seriously? A friendly, happy snapping turtle?

We guessed he must be looking for a handout. It's against the Park rules to feed wild creatures. But he seemed so calm and tame. His hope had him swim to each of us, even coming right out of the water up onto the rocky shore at our feet. He must have been more than half a meter long with a head the size of my fist. He could be fifty years old. His relaxed approach was the only thing that kept April from retreating. Her back was already rammed against the stone backrest, and her feet scrunched close. After entertaining us for almost half an hour, I guess we did not seem quite as entertaining to him, so he wandered away.

Thunder threatened us. Dark clouds in all directions, but the sun kept shining on us. Out came the tarp again and we secured and protected everything from the coming storm. Out came the cards, and we got cozy as we played a few games, wondering when the rain we saw falling across the lake would come and drench us. Booming thunder grew louder and closer. Huge ominous clouds progressively stole our light, and the increased wind robbed our ability to play cards. A lightning show across the lake, and the marching, massive thunderhead clouds captivated our attention.

Hey-O, the freakiest thing happened. No rain fell on us. Miracle. Weird, lovely miracle.

We enjoyed a good campfire out in the open, nice and dry. Even though we felt drowsy, we didn't want to go to sleep on this, our last night. We had to delay the end of our adventure.

*

Sunlight reflected off the water and danced into our tent. The warm aroma of last night's campfire lingered in our hair. The sweet fragrance of pine needles surrounded us. I smelled coffee.

What a glorious sunrise, so Mom told us. April, and I missed it. Dad sat by the water's edge with his buddy, the binoculars.

But none of us hurried that last day. A bright blue sky promised good travelling weather. We had to make the long trek home. We had to leave these awesome backwoods. We had to leave this splendour, this calm peace, this relaxing pace. We must return to the stinky, noisy, busy city.

We definitely have to do this again. Thankfully we had no need for these bear whistles.

But where was the moose?

Good breakfast. Mom complained that we didn't eat enough. Don't all moms do that? She still had too much food to carry back home. I couldn't believe she had enough food for four people for four days in that one medium-sized pack.

Another leisurely coffee while we soaked in the tranquillity and relished the still grandeur of our view.

Well, we finally packed it all up. We had developed a good routine by now. April piled up some wood for the next campers. April knows well the rule of leaving a site better than you find it. If only we all could all live like that and leave the world a better place than we find it. If only.

We loaded up. Checked the area for anything forgotten. We paddled down the long pretty lake. We paused to visit with a family on an appealing peninsula campsite.

Soon we landed at the first portage. Dad seemed to handle it all fine, even with his broken toe. Mom made him remove his water shoes and put on his runners for protection. Mom's sure like to mother.

April and I zipped over this easy short portage and set our gear well off to the side as two incoming canoes offloaded.

Panic on the portage! A horrific scream blasted forth from a little boy who refused to get out of his canoe. What was his problem? We tried hard to hide our giggles from the frustrated dad and embarrassed brothers. This torturous outburst certainly reinforced our resolve never to have children.

We stayed out of their way. This poor dad and grandpa had enough problems.

Mom's yell diverted our attention back down the trail. She just came into view from the first bend in this path. Even though she gasped for breath, she managed to yell, "Are you all right?"

A little puzzled, we called back, "We're fine."

"I heard the screaming and thought there must be a bear mauling someone." Mom stopped when she saw the snivelling boy. She leaned forward with her hands on her thighs and tried to regain control of her frantic breathing.

Travelling with her, back up over the portage for our second load, we helped her hunt for the packs she had flung aside when the shrieking forced her to race to our rescue.

Back in the calm little Hambone Lake, we watched a loaded canoe come from a long narrow bay to our left. As it quickly got closer and closer, their speed bewildered us. Two young children and the two slim trim parents with all their gear in one long canoe, caught and passed us quickly. That's wack. How did they do that? I thought we travelled at a reasonable speed, rapidly crossing the length of this little lake, but they zoomed past us. Whaaaat?

We slowed as we approached our last portage to watch this young family already offloading on shore. The kids grabbed packs and disappeared up the trail. The little mom hoisted a massive backpack which almost knocked her off balance. But then she jogged up after the kids. The short dad also grabbed another big pack and then effortlessly raised the canoe onto his shoulders, and he took off. All of them gone. All their gear gone in one trip. Gone. How did they do that?

We sure didn't move that fast. And why should we? We didn't really want this trip to end….just yet.

On Lake Magnetawan, we slid up to the dock, slowly dragged our gear out, and packed up the cars. Not looking forward to that long, dusty lane. But lunch was a good incentive.

We had lunch all together in Huntsville. A drawn-out farewell.

Four days of canoeing in Algonquin Park's peaceful sanctuary. Weather, no problem. Religious parents, no problem. They prayed before every meal, but I guess there is no harm in thanking a Creator for all the good we experienced in this fresh wilderness. Hard work of paddling and portaging with my little, skinny, noodle arms, no problem. Well, I may have some soreness tomorrow.

Thunder box? No problem.

Let's do it again!

What's That Loud Noise?

Farm Lake to Booth Lake

Written from the point of view of my son, Stephen.

Somehow my Mom finally talked me into a wilderness canoe camping trip. She has a bit of a crazy passion. One of my sisters has gone and survived a four-day trip. Surely, I could survive a two-night, three-day trip. I do like a challenge. Being a bit, okay, a **lot** competitive, I can't let my sister have something over me. But I do like my comforts, hot showers, and comfy chair.

I got my friend, Ed, to come along. Very tall and fit, he should be a good help with the paddling and portaging. My parents had made this short trip before and assured us that this would be a good introduction to a canoeing experience. We started near Farm Lake, north of Madawaska, just east of Algonquin Park's east gate on the main corridor along Highway 60. What a warm, calm day, suitable for soaking up some rays. The Mom warned me about sunburn and sunstroke. Even though I had a painful history of too much sun, I took the opportunity to get tanned.

After paddling up a river, we crossed Farm Lake and then took the short and easy portage to Kitty Lake. This was pretty easy. Portaging? Simple workout.

Out on the water again, we saw nothing but the lake and trees. Bright blue sky and clear waters separated by what looked like endless green wilderness. Maybe this is not as comfortable for two city boys as for my nature-loving Mom. She could eagerly live fifty kilometres into the wilderness surrounded by moose and wolves. City boys are not so calm. But the weather is perfect. Absolutely no wind made paddling a breeze.

We studied the shoreline of Kitty Lake to find the second portage that would take us to Booth Lake. But dense green trees hid any sign of a portage. No path into the forest could be seen. No small yellow sign peeked out between the branches. We kept paddling towards what we assumed to be the correct end of the little lake paddled and then a short way up a river which soon looked totally impassible. The water rushed and splashed over big boulders, and the current tried to push us back to the lake. Finally, we spied the portage sign and small landing area before the path into the dark forest. Now I realized the need for a portage. Navigating in the wilderness is more challenging than a city map, for sure. You certainly need a good sense of direction and a compass.

This second portage proved to be good exercise. No level, smooth walking path this, and I had to watch every step as the rocks and roots made just walking a challenging obstacle course. Muddy areas to tiptoe around and steep inclines added hugely to the workout. Mom warned us that we would have to walk every portage three times. The first time with the backpacks, then back to bring the canoes over.

Mom cautioned us to pack light because she would bring all the cooking gear and all other essentials. We just needed to bring our own clothes and sleeping needs. But my buddy brought the biggest pack, loaded with all kinds of fun gear and fascinating gadgets. He carried the lighter canoe while I helped my dad with the much heavier one. Mom carried the extras. Not so easy to see the precarious footpath with a canoe for a hat.

We had a nice leisurely meandering paddle down the narrows before reaching the big Booth Lake. As we passed a rocky point, we came very, very close to a huge bald eagle who sunbathed on a boulder. Amazed we could get so close, we sat motionlessly and drifted slowly by this majestic bird.

We found a few appealing campsites on the right. All had an easy takeout on sandy beaches. We chose one nearer the center of the lake. What a spectacular view. It's funny that my buddy and I felt somewhat relieved to see other humans paddle past on the rare occasion. We needed the connection to some sign of civilization. We had none other, no cell service, no internet, and no tech of any kind. Exactly how far did the wilderness stretch behind our campsite?

And then I had to ask, "How far into the wilderness do we have to hike to find the thunder box?" I guess that may be the first task when arriving at a campsite. Well, we found the tiny path winding up a hill to the thunder box, hidden in the bush, maybe half a kilometre from shore. Secluded, at least.

We men set up the row of small tents on a good level stretch and put up the tarp, just in case of rain. Mom made lunch and coffee. Yay, coffee. Lunch sure tasted good after almost three hours of paddling and portaging.

We hunted for wood and helped Mom find a suitable tree to hang the food bag. Dad entertained himself with the only toy he was allowed to bring with him. Binoculars. He watched other travellers across the lake and searched the far shore for moose. We all quietly spied on a family of common merganser ducks as they swam by our beach. We followed Mom into the lake for a swim. Of course, no one swam as long or as far as she did. Competitive as I am, I let her win that one.

We explored this pretty site a little. Some trees leaned out over the clear, cool lake, and one made a cute seat. One demanded climbing, so up I went standing on the horizontal trunk, far out over the water. Horizontal trees are the only ones I will climb. Not a fan of heights.

Ed unpacked his huge pack and gave us a show-and-tell of all his cool camping gadgets. A compact stove could boil water quickly with just twigs. Twigs are everywhere, so hunting or chopping is required. It also had a tiny fan to keep the fire going and an energy pack attached, which could power a cell phone, for pictures at least. No cell service out here in the wilderness. Wilderness.

So, what about wildlife? Mom gave us whistles to wear at all times. What now? Not sure I like the sound of that. How does a tiny whistle help? Wolves, bears, moose? They are pretty big!

Mom assured us that Dad's snoring would certainly scare anything away in the night. Just hope I can still sleep. No way was Ed taking that long walk to the thunderbox in the dark alone. I had to go with him in the night to stand guard for him with my long, strong machete. Did I mention that he is a very fit, six-foot-six truck driver? Still, we are city fellas. No 911 gonna work out here.

*

The next day blessed us with warm sunshine again. The bright morning light bounced on the water as we paddled around the lake to the south and glided by tall rock cliffs along the shoreline and around a point to the shallow, grassy bay, hoping to see some wildlife. I guess bullfrogs are wild, but they don't evoke the same excitement as the moose we anticipated. The moose we never saw.

After lunch, curiosity took us exploring, by canoe, up to the far northwest end of the lake wandering along the shoreline to see what the other campsites looked like. Most were vacant, and all appeared level and appealing areas.

We heard a loon call, and call. Searching the lake, we finally saw a lone loon not far from us. Mom and Dad had started to cross the lake and loop back, but Ed and I coasted so slowly towards the beautiful bird and saw a tiny fuzz ball on her back. She kept calling her long call and slowly moved away from us. We stopped so we could continue watching without scaring them away. Soon her calls were answered, and her mate flew into land gracefully beside her. The baby slid from one and quickly climbed aboard the other parent. Amazing!

The family moved away from us, so we parted ways and caught up with my parents. We will never forget that moment of peace and beauty.

Back at our campsite, Mom started supper. We gathered wood for the evening's marshmallow roast.

Suddenly we all froze at a loud noise from behind us, deeper into the forest. Well, we three men froze. Mom never feels fear, and this didn't phase her at all. "What noise? Oh, maybe a beaver took down a tree."

I'm thinking, "Or some bigger creature?" Curiosity got the better of my buddy and me. We took off on a little hike into the forest behind our camp, making enough noise talking, so of course, we saw no wildlife. Thankfully.

Not long after, Mom had to take the hike to the thunderbox. We all wondered, "But what about whatever made that noise?"

We silently cheered when she re-emerged from the tiny trail.

But she did have a story of a wildlife encounter. She calmly recounted, "I raised the lid of the thunderbox and was just about to sit when I saw a mouse run across the front edge of the seat. I had to tell him to hurry on his way as I didn't want to sit on him."

My Mom is not afraid of anything. Weird, eh?

In shock, Ed exclaimed, "If that had been me seeing that mouse, I would have screamed like a twelve-year-old girl."

My Mom laughed so loud at this. My Mom laughs embarrassingly loud quite easily.

We played cards, but darkness soon made that impossible. Dad told us the murder mystery story of the famous Canadian artist Tom Thomson as we roasted marshmallows.

*

The bright sun woke us early. How lucky are we to get three days of perfect weather? We leisurely ate our big breakfast and then packed everything up. Not fun, knowing our time here in this tranquillity neared its conclusion.

Mom took off with her big pack when we reached the first and most challenging portage. Ed felt determined to finish his work in one crossing, so he hoisted up his heavy pack and the lighter canoe, and off he went. Dad and I grabbed our packs to follow him. As Mom returned for her second load, she met my tall buddy dripping with sweat and breathing hard. In concern, she tried to encourage him, "You are almost at the end of the portage. You can make it."

He did make it, dropped his loads, and sat in the cool by the water's edge to recuperate. When the rest of us had finished our last trip across the portage, he confessed to my Mom, "I felt so drained I thought I would die. Your motivation kept me from collapsing on the spot."

I had to giggle and give Mom credit for not responding with, "I told you so."

We took our time paddling through the narrow winding river and watched otters swim in front of us and then stand on the shore to observe us as we glided by. But a little further on, as we maneuvered through the shallow water and thick grasses, Ed shrieked and almost jumped out of our canoe when he saw a massive snapping turtle inches from his hand.

This set my Mom laughing, "Oh, there's that twelve-year-old girl again!"

Dark clouds moved in as we reached the end of our canoe trip. Just after we loaded up all our gear and headed out of Algonquin Park, noisy thunder announced the arrival of hard rain.

We had lunch together at a tiny restaurant back in Madawaska on Highway 60. Ed and I sure enjoyed our time back in the wilderness. Fun time with good company. Just enough of a challenge and perfect weather.

A lightning show concluded our perfect canoeing adventure. A trip to remember. Peaceful memories, a happy place to help us and calm us through the storms of life.

I just might go on another one of these canoe trips.

I wonder if Mom can convince my younger brothers to come on a canoe camping adventure?

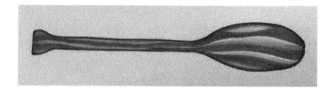

Rain or Shine.

Canoe Lake to Little Doe Lake

Yay, Linda, my Judo buddy, finally agreed to come on a canoe trip with me. We have been friends for years. We met at a Judo class and worked well together. We became a team, teaching kinder fitness, ladies' self-defence, and Judo classes together for over fifteen years. She is always cheerful and so much fun to be with.

But then I moved far away. We wanted to keep close, so I organized our first camping trip to Algonquin Park. She had never been camping, so I found an old ranger's cabin on Rain Lake on the west side of Algonquin Park north of Huntsville. I knew two other ladies who also wanted to try camping in Algonquin Park. Since they eagerly agreed to try canoeing, I rented two canoes and the cabin for three nights. This whole story is found in "Here We are Ladies."

What a wonderful time we had, so for the next two years, we four ladies rented a yurt on Mew Lake. The year after those in the yurt, Linda and I used my little pop-up A-frame trailer, and we camped at Pog Lake one year and Tea Lake campground another summer.

Finally, she eagerly agreed to try a canoe trip. I wanted to find something not too long, not too many portages with easy access—this time.

We took off at Canoe Lake, the busiest spot in all of Algonquin Park. The gift store, restaurant, and canoe rental are crowded with summer visitors.

You can rent a canoe for just a few hours or a couple of weeks. The well over one hundred vehicles tightly packed into the parking lot for canoe trippers, prove how popular this jump-off spot into the wilderness is. Near the rear of the store, showers wait for those returning to civilization from a long canoe trip.

This is one of the few lakes with cottages, allows motorboats, and is the home of three kids' camps. My husband's dream job would be to give Tom Thomson murder mystery tours around the lake on a pontoon boat. Of course, my dream job would be to take people on wilderness canoe trips. So here I go.

My buddy and I took off through the crowd and passed many as we traversed the lake to the north end. We followed the narrow bay to the right. We had to be careful of sunken deadheads here, which are large old logs left behind from the logging days.

Oh, don't be fooled. Logging still happens in the park but is mostly hidden from summer visitors. Down the roads to the less used access points are huge signs warning, "Beware of Logging Trucks."

We reached the short, level portage and waited for an opening on the shore to land. Watching all the other paddlers can be quite educational or humorous, to see what they try to bring with them. Some even bring coolers. How do you carry a cooler over a portage or hang it in the tree at night?

At the end of the portage, we reloaded and glided back into the water. With similar strength and rhythmic, synchronized strokes, we paddled well together, increasing speed. Most of the other travellers headed right. We went straight north. An informative, clear waterproof map with a compass set right in front of the navigator is essential to find your way along even the simplest of routes.

We crossed another lake and passed another busy kids' camp. As we entered the narrow north end of Teepee Lake, we hunted for a campsite. Should we be on the right or left side? Do we want the morning light waking us or the west sky view? I just hope the thunderbox is well-hidden.

*

The next morning looked like another lovely day as we continued north to Little Doe Lake. Here we found a campsite with the **best** view. Perched high on a hill, we had a panoramic view of the lovely lake. Linda enjoyed calling down to passing trippers to learn where they were headed and how long their trip would be.

We set up camp and hunted for wood and a good tree to hang the food bag. Not an easy job to find a tree with a strong, long branch, high enough and far enough away from other trees and branches. But we made a fabulous discovery. A cable had been positioned between two tall trees with a hook and a winch. How easy is that?

*

The following morning, clouds covered the sky, but after breakfast, we headed down a short river and struggled over a beaver dam to explore Tom Thomson Lake. We climbed up the large smooth rock on the far west shore and had lunch. Another lovely view.

We managed to return to our campsite on Little Doe Lake before the drizzle began. Dry and happy under our tarp, we drank hot tea and played cards. A few paddlers slipped past us, hurrying to their next destination.

When Doug and I had camped here a couple of years before, we watched moose on the far shore. But we saw none this time.

The rain looked like it would give us a break, so we took off to explore the winding river to the little Blue Jay Lake. Lots of grasses and bulrushes hid ducks and a great blue heron. What a blessing to take our time to explore the wonderful wilderness and catch a glimpse of the beautiful wildlife.

Treasures can be found all around our campsite, beauty in every variety of unique flower and plant.

I love toadstools and am compelled to take pictures of them. There are thousands of different wild mushrooms in Ontario of such unique shapes and colours.

More drizzle fell as we made supper under our tarp. We slept dry and so well in the silent total darkness. We always remembered to keep a flashlight, whistle, and toilet paper within reach for any night trips down the tiny trail to the thunderbox.

*

No rain threatened to bother us on our last day. After a leisurely breakfast, we had to pack up and return to Canoe Lake. We didn't want to leave.

Canoeing is not so much about the destination; it's the journey, especially on the last day. I wanted to take my time and experience the beauty. We watched the shore for a possible moose or any other critter.

114

We waved to some campers and then noticed high up at the pinnacle of a tall tree, perched a great blue heron. What? I thought I would only find them in the weedy shallow waters.

What a good trip, rain or shine. What a good friend. Thanks so much for coming canoeing with me, Linda.

Family Time

Rock Lake to Pen Lake

Our oldest son, Stephen, and his new bride, Heather, actually accepted my invitation to come on a canoe trip with Doug and me. They had recently returned from their big luxurious, fancy honeymoon to Greece. I sure hoped they could enjoy this wilderness experience. My joy doubled when our eldest daughter, April, and her partner, Chris, agreed to join us as well.

Most people my age enjoy retirement and go glamping with their huge RVs or fifth wheels or cruise to an exotic destination. But we don't have that kind of money or any money, so we take our cruise trips in a canoe into our Canadian wilderness in between our multiple part-time jobs. Poor Doug, canoe trips into the wilderness have become my obsession.

I thank God daily for my five kids and now my kids' partners, too. Heather loves to laugh, play games, hike, and go to all kinds of sports games with Stephen. She has done lots of camping with family and friends, in group camping, with lots of little tents all huddled together in big campgrounds with comfort stations or at least outhouses. She had never heard of a thunderbox that I warned her would be at wilderness campsites. I am sure she wondered, "Just how private is a box out in the open when camping with five other people? Just how far into the forest wilderness do I have to hike to find this box?"

There are other considerations when camping in the wilderness. Weather? Wild weather? Wildlife? What would we eat? How do we keep wildlife from eating our food? I told everyone how the little red squirrels and chipmunks threaten our food more than lynxes, wolves, and bears. Oh my!

I assured them how we could take precautions. We would all have to wear a whistle at all times. I am unsure if this reassured them or caused them to wonder if we need it "at all times."

And food? I sure hoped Heather would like the meals I packed. Three days of vegan foods. Veggies are much easier to pack and keep than meat and dairy of any kind. Maybe it would be less appealing to the wolves and bears. There's a bonus.

Since I looked after all the cooking gear and food, my kids just needed to pack their sleeping bags, minimal clothing and tents. I had to remind them to bring a sun hat and rain gear. A Mama has to do things like that. I sure hope it doesn't rain. Personally, I don't care what the weather does, but I am sure they will enjoy their trip with me if it is sunny.

So, the day arrived bright and warm. April and Chris loaded their canoe with their two small packs, and Stephen and Heather had bigger bags. With all three canoes loaded, we pushed off from shore. Our trip began on a little river that meandered out to Rock Lake, taking us so close to an elegant great blue heron who stood motionless, ready to attack some unsuspecting fish or frog. I guess herons aren't vegan.

The calm, bright day made crossing this lake enjoyable, and we easily reached the southwest side to glide alongside the tall rock cliffs. Now the name Rock Lake makes sense. Of course, Stephen took far too many selfies with the rock face as a gorgeous background, causing the rest of us paddlers to wait. April and Chris like to forget about their phones as much as possible.

Stephen announced at the beginning that we were not going to race, no competition. But I don't know. Sometimes it seemed like he and his sister might have had some rivalry. Who would make it to that portage at the far south end of the lake first? I had been there before, so at least I knew where to go, but since the lake narrowed to a definite end, it proved easy to find.

Portaging seemed more complicated than some anticipated, I bet. Step out of the canoe into the water. Drag it ashore. Take out all the packs. Put on shoes. Grab a backpack and paddles, and life jackets. Head off into the forest. Portages are usually not much of a trail but a narrow path over rocks and roots, down into swampy areas, up and down and winding this way and that. Finally, we could see through to Penn Lake. When we headed back for the canoes, I led my family down a barely visible path to view the reason for the portage. The small river that joins the two lakes splashed over rocks and down a waterfall. So pretty. Of course, this made for another good photo shoot.

It took a bit of coordination for Stephen and Heather to carry the canoe tandem. April managed hers by herself. Impressive.

After reloading, we took off down this long lake. So quiet. So beautiful. Surrounding us stood vibrant green trees, oh-so-clear water below, and brilliant blue sky above.

We could see no one else. It appeared that we had the whole lake to ourselves. But occasionally, we spotted a canoe half hidden on the shore and a camp sign near it. The shore alternated between soft sand and huge boulders. What would we find at our campsite? When would we find our campsite? Surely lunchtime had come and gone.

I announced that I hoped the next campsite would be vacant as I had been here the previous year and found it perfect for our three tents. Amazingly it was free and proved to be better than my kids had expected. It had a good-sized level area with a big stone fire pit and log benches, which most sites have. But this site had the bonus of being on a peninsula. Behind the fire pit stood a steep ridge with tall skinny red pines and a soft aromatic pine needle floor. I showed them the sun-warmed, soft, white beach down the other side. This surprise bonus surely pleased them all.

We quickly and easily found three good, level spots for our three tents. Doug chose the spot near the fire pit for us. April took the top of the ridge, and Stephen got the beach. As they set up, I made lunch and coffee and tea. I brought a fun variety of fruity and herbal teas just for my new daughter.

We had such a relaxing time lying on the beach. I swam long and far. Stephen, missing his shower, had to jump in at least briefly. The rest preferred the warm sand instead of the chilly water. I am sure the clarity of these lakes amazed them all. **So** clean, as opposed to the murky waters of southern Ontario that my kids had become accustomed to. I bet these transparent waters reminded Heather of her childhood on Lake Superior.

Stephen's obsession kicked in. He made a tall inuksuk on the beach. He made one on the stony shore on the other side of the peninsula, one on a boulder, another near the canoes, more in the nearby bay and yet another near the campfire. Well, of course, his sister had to show a bit of competitiveness and made a few as well.

The thunderbox turned out better than my kids had feared. Not too far, not too stinky, and just enough seclusion. April hunted for wood, and Chris helped hunt for a tree for the food bag. They had done this before. Doug filtered and sterilized water to fill all our water bottles and the pot for supper's soup and more tea and coffee.

The evening gave us time for marshmallows and stories. Well, someone had to ask Dad to tell Heather about the murder mystery of Tom Thomson. That is his obsession.

*

Thick morning mist caused the couple on the beach to wonder what had happened to the world. Dense, damp fog encompassed them.

Doug disappeared into the mist as he paddled out from shore, hoping to find cooler water to refill all our containers. Every season, day, and moment surprises me with wondrous beauty. Thank-you Creator, Father.

The night had been chilly, and we all laughed at Chris's announcement, "I thought our bed at home is crowded sleeping with Mabel (British bulldog) and Clark (cat). But April was so cold last night that she squished herself into my sleeping bag with me."

After breakfast, we all eagerly leaped into our canoes and paddled to the far end of the lake. We hunted the west shore for the creek that the map told us would lead to a waterfall. But the low water level had turned the creek into a tiny stream, far too small and shallow for canoes.

We continued to the south end of the lake, examining the shoreline until we could finally spy the portage sign. The smooth, slippery rock sure makes exiting a canoe treacherous. Yet very amusing to watch the others try. Leaving our canoes pulled up, out of the way on the smooth rock shore, we hiked across to have a view of Clydegale Lake.

The pretty sight made me wish we had more days to continue our trip, but our two nights were booked on Pen Lake, so we retraced our steps. On our way along the rocky path, we gathered up good-sized branches that lay along the path for our evening's campfire. We needed extra because a camping rule is, "Leave a campsite better than you find it." Which means cleaner and with a good pile of wood for the next campers.

Two days full of sunshine and paddling. I had warned them about too much sun. "Please wear hats and long, thin sleeves to prevent sunburn or sunstroke." Do kids ever listen to Mama? Maybe not. They wanted nice tans. They didn't want ugly hats. So, there you go. By evening, two had bad sunburns, and one had mild sunstroke. I pulled out my first aid kit and did a bit of doctoring. Whatever I could. I hoped the aloe vera, lots of water, and a good sleep would help heal them.

*

Morning gave us no hint of rain. But thankfully, the thin clouds might prevent more hazards. We had a slow lazy morning, and then we packed up. Off we headed back down the lake and over the portage.

We took it easier on this return trip as one still suffered a little from sunstroke. No competition this time. But the growing wind gave us enough challenge anyway.

The blue heron still stood guarding the entrance to the river. So stately.

Once we made it to the dock at the end of our trip and had all our gear and canoes packed up, our three cars convoyed down to the Canoe Lake restaurant. Good meal, cold drinks with lots of ice, laughs, and pictures. What a wonderful family time.

I am so thankful for the excellent weather, God's amazing creation, and my fun family. I wonder if they will come with me again.

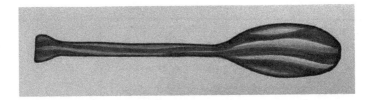

Attacked!

Kioshkokwi Lake to Laurel Lake

God has blessed me with a very talented and generous husband. Doug gifted me with the promise that he would go on a six-day canoe trip with me. Finally. I felt such excitement, and I immediately unfolded my new Algonquin Park canoe routes map. My old one had become shredded with overuse.

Doug had joined me on various short three-day canoe trips in the past few years. Doug and I had camped on Ralph Bice Lake, David Lake, Little Doe Lake, Tom Tomson Lake, Booth Lake, and Ragged Lake and more.

Where to go this time? Where could we go that would be new to us? I had to plan so our daily paddling would not be too long or the portages too difficult. I surely didn't want Doug to regret having agreed to do this. I bought him a better mattress and made sure we had room for his tiny camping chair, binoculars, and his newest astronomy magazine.

Finally, the day came for our big trip. Oh, I know that six days is a short trip for most wilderness explorers, but it was long for us. We reached the Kiosk campground office bright and early that July morning.

Most of our route lay beside an old Canadian Northern Railway line that William MacKenzie and Donald Mann completed building in 1915 and ran from Ottawa to Sudbury. In 1923 it became part of the Canadian National Railway and ran until 1995. Both railway lines that ran through

Algonquin Park serviced lumber camps and sawmills, such as the one owned by Sydney Staniforth, which operated from 1936 until 1973 at Kiosk. The railways helped establish communities long before roads came close. When road construction allowed vehicle traffic, some of these almost self-sufficient settlements along the rail line became ghost towns. There are no rails now, but the flat rail bed is easily visible, and we crossed its path a few times.

When getting our permits, I asked if most of the campsites would be filled. She explained that the bugs had scared away many campers. I thought they must be city people because we had not been bothered by mosquitoes in many years.

Heading east, we paddled under the rail trestle and easily found the first portage at the east end of Lake Kioshkokwi. Then we hauled our gear over the first and longest of our portages which crossed over the rail bed. We quickly realized why some campers may have turned around right there and retreated home. The mosquitoes attacked us, covered our arms and necks, crawled under our hats, into our ears, and up our noses, and caused uncontrolled coughing. Breathing hard on this portage had caused us to suck in many of the tiny vampires. We doused each other with bug repellant for our return trip to get the rest of our gear and the canoe. But if we could have had a bath in the repellant, I am sure it would have made no difference. These hordes of assailants relentlessly tormented us. Quickly we finished the gruelling hike, threw our gear and ourselves into the canoe, and escaped on the open waters of Mink Lake.

I will bet Doug must have thought, "And I agreed to this for six days? How will we survive?" He must have wished we had turned and fled for home as others surely had. But he knew that one of my favourite quotes is, "Never give up, never surrender."

He may have insisted that we turn around if he had only known I brought only a tiny amount of repellant. We had encountered so few bugs for so many years that I had not imagined we would need much, if any. Shhhhh. Our secret.

We peacefully sailed on Little Mink Lake, following the rail line on the west shore. Somewhere buried in the regrowth of trees hid more remnants of another town called Ascalon.

Another shorter portage brought us to the longer Mink Lake. We found a beautiful campsite on a high peninsula about halfway down this lake. Tall red pines allowed the breeze to blow over the open area and kept the bugs away. But then we had to hunt for the thunderbox. Oh bother. Far, far down the densely wooded path sat the torture box. Those nasty bugs have now gone where no bugs have ever gone before. Oh, my.

We set our tent on the highest level spot and used a big flat boulder as a table for my tiny stove. Lunch and coffee. Yay. Time to relax, nap, and read.

This campsite had a perfect little beach which allowed easy access for swimming. I always must swim. Floating on the cool waters feels wonderful, especially after our morning's workout and bug battle.

Only twigs fire my little camp stove. Twigs abound everywhere. No chopping is required. Pinecones will work, too, and are always excellent fire starters. Doug and I rarely make a campfire. We enjoy total darkness, which enables us to study the stars. My astronomer-husband loves these sparkling skies, and our lovely open beach made a good viewpoint. We lay on the soft sand and hunted for constellations and meteors. But it didn't take long before those nasty vampires forced us to race to our tent. Good night.

*

A gorgeous, sunny morning greeted us. After breakfast, we packed up and headed out on our day's journey, hoping we could find another site so open and breezy, and free of bugs.

We found the portage to Cauchon Lake at the south end of Mink Lake. Here we crossed the rail bed again. The remains of the town of Mink Lake hid somewhere in the trees near this portage.

Paddling east, this wider lake allowed a nice breeze. We saw no one else but could easily see the rail bed along the north shore. As we reached the end of the lake, we could not see any opening to the river connecting to Little Cauchon Lake. We slowed and studied the shore. The rail bed appeared to run along this shore, and bushes grew thick everywhere. Not knowing where to go, we just kept approaching the very end point and finally saw the tiny opening under the train trestle, obscured by thick bushes. We barely squeezed through. In the water below, I could see that the beavers had been busy, and I told Doug, "By the time we make our return trip, the beavers will make this a difficult climb over."

We followed the meandering grassy creek, which took us under another bridge before it opened up to Little Cauchon Lake. Thinking we were deep in the wilderness, the sight of three houses really surprised me. This must be evidence of another town the train had helped found, called Daventry. They looked ancient and charming. Curiosity tempted us to explore, but we stayed the course.

We did stop at an empty campsite on a big smooth sun-warmed rock for lunch. I didn't want to tell Doug how tired I felt and how much I hoped lunch would rejuvenate me.

I had planned that we would travel the longest distance on this day. But now I have finally learned that my second day of paddling should be easier than the rest. I finally realized that I always expend way too much energy just being **so** excited on the first day. I should plan my second day to be the easiest day. Silly me.

After lunch, we headed down the last half of the lake. It grew steadily narrower, and the wind gave us a gentle push. I surely needed it as I had run out of energy. I rigged up an umbrella in front of me on one side of the bow to catch the wind as a sail, and I just had to use my paddle on the other side as a rudder. Doug also took a needed break from paddling and refilled out water bottles.

The lake ended at our last portage of the day and the shortest one of our trip. But we quickly learned this would be challenging. The rocky incline turned mid-way into a very steep, treacherous decline.

At the base lay a mess of boulders to maneuver around. It is pretty tricky to get into the canoe without sliding off the slippery rocks into the deep water. As wobbly kneed as we felt, we did succeed.

We took our time to view this lovely Laurel Lake and hoped the island in the center would have a vacant campsite. We had seen no other paddlers all day and no one on this lake either.

Gulls greeted us as we paddled towards the island. Right out at midpoint, between shores, they stood on the water. Well, it sure looked like that. They were not floating or sitting on the water but stood there as we approached, warning us of submerged rocks. These unseen boulders surely would have hung us up or tipped us over if we had not had the help of these neighbours. Thanks guys.

With renewed excitement, we climbed up onto this island and surveyed our new home. Tall red and white pines. Open and breezy. Maybe too windy as it appeared a huge tree must have come down recently, laying right across the open fire pit area.

Now, where is that thunderbox? This island is a little small. Oh. There we go. This fully exposed thunderbox perched on the highest point with a beautiful panoramic view of the entire lake. Thankfully we had the whole lake to ourselves. But every trip up here would be preceded with, "Avert your eyes, please."

Time to make coffee and lunch, then set up camp. We found a perfect spot for the hammock. We never hang it very high and always place the life jackets underneath. Safety precautions. Always look for ways to stay safe so you do not have to learn the same painful lessons we have endured.

We found a good flat area for the tent. But what if there are a couple of good spots? Doug and I inevitably have quite the discussion. Oh, bother. How can something so simple become so complicated? The tent needs level land, hopefully with no protruding rocks or roots. Not near a leaning tree. Not near the tallest tree. Not totally exposed. Not close to the shore, or in a hollow, or you may awake in a puddle. Some campsites have a few good tent spots, others may have only one. Good luck.

Sleep comes so easily for me when camping. The best ever. But the path to the thunderbox became treacherous in the dark night, perched beside a twenty-foot cliff that dropped to boulders on the north shore of our island. But I love the dark and the silence, and the challenge.

*

The early morning call of loons awoke us to dense fog. But the warm sun soon cleaned it away. We had the entire day to relax, recuperate, and enjoy this little paradise. Eating, reading, napping, watching two canoes cross the lake from one end and disappear down the portage, being entertained by gulls and loons and a graceful great blue heron, who swooped around to land in the water at the far end of our island. I swam around the island a couple of times. Doug sat on the sun-warmed smooth rock on the shore with his feet in the water, at least. We thought we might take a little trip exploring the portage to the north, but we chose to be lazy and enjoy our island.

Ravens came by for a visit. What a noisy pair. We could hear them approaching long before they appeared over the forest across the lake. It seemed to me like a demanding child following his busy mother. "Maaam. Maaam. Maaam." And then the loud, raspy, annoyed response, "Whaaat?" This sequence repeated louder and louder until the pair came to rest in the tall treetops above our heads. Maybe our activities entertained them for a while. Mom took off while the insistent child followed closely with constant shouts.

We played cards until the wind arrived. It grew stronger and stronger. We had to go to bed early. "If we don't get in that tent, this gale will take it away."

Thankfully we did not blow off the island. No trees fell on us, and only a little rain. Morning came bright and sunny again. What a peaceful retreat we had in this pretty little paradise.

Too soon, we had to pack up and head out. I like to take my time on a canoe trip, enjoy the time and, place, and experience. Doug seems to love to get a job done. As he says, "It is all about the destination, not the journey." I think that he may have dreaded the thoughts of the very steep

140

incline on the portage so soon into our day's travel. But he is big, strong, and a good sport.

We would not have too far to go today. We paddled down the length of Little Cauchon Lake and the grassy river. But getting into Cauchon Lake proved just as I predicted. The beavers had been busy, and we had to wiggle, push, and scrape our way over the growing dam through the narrow passageway beneath the trestle. Since I sat at the front, I couldn't see Doug crying at all the paint being scratched off our new, costly canoe.

Halfway down this lake, we found a nice campsite. All the campsites we passed looked inviting and vacant, and it appeared we had the entire lake to ourselves again.

Loons live on every Algonquin Lake I have visited. On the rare occasion, they have allowed us to get quite close. So gorgeous.

On one trip, we had to come to a sudden stop. Okay, I mean a sudden switch from powerful strokes to back paddling. A loon had surfaced twenty feet in front of us, too busy with his lunch to be afraid of our nearness. Our quick detour to glide around him gave us an excellent close-up view of this beautiful bird—intricate patterns, long and sleek.

Today Doug picked our new campsite because of the huge smooth rock shore. A perfect perch for him to view the whole lake with a gentle breeze and zero bugs.

We may only cover a little distance in one day, but then we have time to relish the journey and each site. Then we have time to set up and enjoy our hammock. Oh, I do like a challenge, but I don't like exhaustion. I love a good workout, but I want my husband to join me again.

Which reminds me. I pack very minimally. But I had to consent to bring a couple of luxuries for Doug. A good yet tiny camp chair. And I usually bring tiny binoculars, but for this longer trip, I allowed him to bring his big, heavy Astro-binoculars.

The fire pit sat protected from the wind behind the boulder with a flat log bench. A tiny cook stove needs a gentle breeze to keep the flame going, but too much wind steals the heat before it reaches the pot.

We found a good level grassy area for the tent and the flat rail bed just beyond that. What an excellent opportunity for a hike. But hordes of torturous deer flies attacked us immediately, turning our leisurely stroll into a sprint back to the rocky shore. Mosquitoes are annoying, but deer flies drive you insane, zinging around and around and around until they finally take a painful chunk out of you. So, no hike today. Boohoo. More time for a swim. Yay.

This campsite had an unusual thunderbox. This box had walls like an outhouse but no door. It sat far too close to shore, and the path took us over washed-out giant tree roots, which looked like an ankle injury waiting to happen. I definitely needed my flashlight that night.

*

A bright sunny morning greeted us again. We headed back to Mink Lake and hoped for the same open peninsula campsite. Since we had seen only two other canoes in the past two days, we thought our chances would be pretty good.

As we approached the portage, Cauchon Lake narrowed with rock cliffs on one side. A bird hidden in the dense forest awed us with its intricate song. Spectacular scenery, splendid song, warm sunshine, clean, fresh air. We just wanted to be still, drink in all the beauty, and give thanks to the One who created it all.

We made it back to our first campsite. Yay! Little soft, warm breezy beach. I must repeat "breezy" often, as it pushed the millions of mosquitoes back into the forest.

We watched two canoes pass by and take the next site. Most of these wilderness sites are so far apart that you can rarely see or hear anyone at them. But we could see these guys as they jumped into the water for a swim from their rocky shore.

We felt so blessed with such good weather. I could not believe so few other adventurers travelled here. Doug felt sure the bombardment of bugs on that first longer portage had turned them back.

I had lots of time to swim. I felt so happy in the serenity. Such a wonderful time to be rejuvenated and experience the calm that only comes within the green living wilderness of God's creation. Here is the best place to witness His artistry and some of His peace that is beyond our understanding.

Then some sadness crept in, realizing that tomorrow we had to leave.

Just before we began our trip, I bought Doug a comfy mattress. I know it should have been high quality, compact and expensive, but I am too cheap and poor. But at least it was comfy until this our last night. Now it leaked. Of course, I offered mine, but he refused. It is far too tiny for him. I did whatever I could to make something he could sleep on. I scooped up piles of the soft orange pine needles, covered them with our life jackets, towels, and then the folded flat mattress. Ta da: a bed. Maybe? Oh well, I tried.

*

On our last day, we thought the most challenging part would be the portage. Paddling is so easy. The rhythmic strokes are so calming. For me, it feels as though I am being restored, like tuning a piano: everything in life, in health, in thoughts, seems to function more harmoniously.

We met a very fit young lady as we began that last portage. By young, I mean maybe thirty-five. She solo carried a heavy canoe. Behind her struggled a few teenage girls with huge packs. We wondered how these pretty girls would even endure this first portage of their long trip. I know that style far outweighs safety or comfort for teen girls. But considering this was wilderness camping and we had met very few people these six days, this fashion show of short skirts, shorter shorts, and very skimpy swimsuits surprised us. We honestly didn't think they would survive the assault of the mad mob of mosquitoes that would surely soon devour them on this trail.

But we survived. We survived six days of insane bugs and were blessed with beautiful weather in this peaceful paradise. Even Doug survived without his geeky gadgets and comfy bed.

We only had to cross part of Lake Kioshkokwi. This first bay grew windy and wavy. Soon we reached the passageway under the trestle, and the last jaunt should take us just fifteen minutes.

But.

As we turned to pass under the trestle, huge waves forced us back, threatening to capsize us. We tried again. Wild wind and white-capped waves refused to let us through. We hauled up on shore behind the opening and considered our options. The strength of the wind and waves proved too powerful for our paddling. To get through this narrow passageway, we could walk along the shore, dragging the loaded canoe. But the slippery rocks would make an ankle injury too easy. And then, we would still have to fight white-capped waves which would slam us broadside. So now what do we do?

I am a good swimmer, enjoy the water, and am unable to sink, so waves do not scare me. I like a good challenge. But these massive whitecaps took it way past a challenge.

I know Doug is uneasy with any wind. He cannot swim. Even though he is a very strong paddler, we must avoid danger.

We need challenges. We need to keep safe.

Sitting on the rocky lakeside at the base of this old bridge, we knew that this rail bed above us led to the Kiosk access point. It would be a long, hot hike infested with deer flies. But at least level and straight. First, we had to haul all our gear up the steep embankment. We rested while watching the lake's power and snacked on nuts. After a well-needed drink of water, we took off with our first load. Even though it took longer than expected, we felt relieved to have this rail bed to hike instead of the hazardous struggle on the lake. Hot and tired, we headed back for the canoe and the rest of our gear. I felt happy about our safety and the excellent workout. I know Doug kept going with the thought of a tall icy drink waiting for him at the restaurant on the drive home.

We made it. Relaxed, we savoured a late leisurely lunch. This popular restaurant in Mattawa had cheerful staff but very few options for us vegans. We do fancy French fries, and Doug sat so content with his tall glass of pop and another of ice water.

We did it, six days in the wonderful wilderness. I am so thankful for my generous husband and the amazing Creator of this peaceful paradise, Algonquin Park.

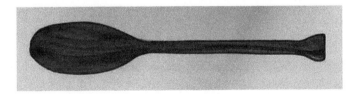

Awesome View.

Smoke Lake to Ragged Lake

Linda and I had been emailing for weeks, excitedly counting down the days until our canoe trip. Our annual camping trip had finally arrived. Last year we had to go back to car camping due to Linda's wrist injury. Instead of paddling lakes, we hiked to the highest point in Algonquin Park on the Centennial Ridges trail. What fabulous lookouts.

But this year, with her wrist healed, her excitement for paddling almost equalled mine. She sat on the dock at Smoke Lake, holding the canoe so I could load all our gear.

Bright, warm sun and no wind. How perfect is that?

We headed for the portage to Ragged Lake. Our excitement made our heavy backpacks feel light. Rocky shores, towering trees, calm seas, and this beautiful day made the hunt for a vacant campsite a fun adventure, like searching for treasure.

We stopped at one empty site and climbed the steep bank to explore a little, but we wanted to paddle further, so we only stayed for a short time. Ragged Lake has long bays and big islands dotted with a good variety of campsites. As we approached the portage to Big Porcupine Lake, we found a large site perched up high with an excellent, open, westerly view. Tall pines, stony beach, nice flat campfire pit with a natural bench/ledge on the side of the hill.

On such a slope, it surprised us to find a very level spot for Linda's tent. I brought my new hammock to try out, so we found two sturdy trees with lots of choices with well-spaced trees everywhere.

We tried out a new challenge. Linda eagerly took my phone and videoed me as I walked through our campsite, explaining how to find a good spot to pitch a tent. Oh my, that first attempt at getting onto YouTube proved fun. Linda made a good coach and held the camera so steadily. But I think she would have been the better person to be seen on the video, and I should have been hidden behind the camera. She is much younger and prettier.

After setting up camp, we had to jump in the lake for a swim. By swim, I do not mean wade or walk in hip-deep water, and we swim far out in the deep, clear waters. So rejuvenating.

We stayed on the same site for three nights and took day trips to explore.

*

The next morning, we checked out the neighbouring site, which no one occupied. With a big soft beach so close to a vast swamp, we wondered if it had many moose visiting.

We paddled through the swamp in search of the portage south. I found it so puzzling that we saw no ducks, frogs, turtles, or moose in this vast boggy bay. We have not seen a moose in our seven years of camping together. Linda has concluded that they are just a myth. They must not really exist. I assured her that they do exist. I have even shown her my collection of many moose photos that I have indeed taken within

Algonquin Park's broad borders. But she refuses to believe it since she has never seen any herself.

We hiked over the portage just to have a look at Big Porcupine Lake. Or should I say ran? Being a city gal, Linda found the bugs intolerable and had to warn others exiting their canoes to put their bug repellant on. Silly city folk.

*

The next afternoon, the rain kept us under my tarp, playing games and watching a chipmunk. I had placed a tiny bar of soap, a small towel, and a filled expandable water jug with a spout by the path to the thunderbox. But the pretty rodent stole the soap and carried it up the hill. How could he possibly find that tasty? Yuck!

Later, when the rain finally allowed us, we hiked along the shore till the dense brush blocked our way. So much beauty in every place we looked: tiny ferns growing out of huge boulders, oh-so-soft moss in the hollows, bright white birch trees framed by vibrant green spruce trees, brilliant yellow toadstools, cute tiny toads, and erratic butterflies.

Did you know that there are five thousand different mushrooms and fungi in Ontario and eighty different kinds of butterflies in Algonquin Park? Amazing. Some are artistically decorated with gorgeous colours; others are camouflaged into hiding. Keep looking for all the hidden treasures.

Surely now you will have to admit that you feel the passion for exploring all the wonders in this Ontario wilderness.

I had told Linda too many stories of paddling in large lakes with huge waves, so she felt determined that we leave extra early on our last morning. We hoped to avoid the afternoon winds on our return trip across Smoke Lake. But we didn't want to leave at all.

*

We awoke to a vanished world. We could see nothing. Dense fog hid everything beyond one meter in front of us. Don't hurry. Walk carefully. A four-meter-tall cliff ran along most of our water's edge.

We had an easy breakfast of protein bars. By the time we had packed up our gear and loaded everything in the canoe, the sun had transformed the fog into a brilliant blue sky.

Retracing our travels, the view all looked entirely different from this perspective. Beauty everywhere and friendly fellow canoeists to greet.

A happy camper eagerly called to us as we drifted past his campsite. He readied himself to leap off the tall rocky point into the cool, clear water. What fun. What freedom.

Come, and catch the rejuvenating enthusiasm for canoe camping.

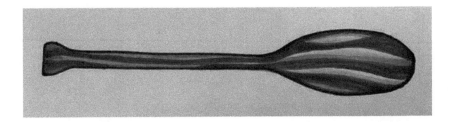

Will Anyone Believe Us?

Little Otter Slide Lake

What an unusual spring. Minimal rainfall caused a total fire ban in Algonquin Park at the beginning of June. A fire ban means no outdoor fires and no campfires anywhere. The only exception is if you are wilderness camping without a camp stove. But you must make your fire only for cooking and thoroughly extinguish it afterward. Keep wood, all twigs, and pine needles swept far from the fire pit.

Doug and I headed out early for our first canoe trip of the year. Although rain threatened, who cares? With great anticipation, I sat smiling in the car the entire one-and-a-half-hour drive to our access point at Canoe Lake.

I had booked five canoe trips for this summer. Due to Covid, the opening of the park had been delayed until today.

Soon after we entered Algonquin Park through the east gate, Doug suddenly put the car flashers on and pulled over. Two moose stood eating in the swampy area not far from the road. We had to take pictures of these massive creatures.

By 8:00 am, we loaded our canoe and pushed off of the beach in the slight drizzle. By the look of the almost empty parking lot, we may have been the first paddlers to head out on a canoe trip from this access.

A second couple came up behind us as we crossed the portage from Canoe Lake to Joe Lake. They headed north to their destination of Little Doe Lake. We headed east to Burnt Island Lake.

When we reached the far swampy end of Little Joe Lake, we slowed and paddled totally silently through the lily pads as I took pictures of the cow moose and her calf with my new camera. What a privilege to be so close to these massive wild animals. Of course, they saw us. Mama tried to ignore us, but her yearling seemed distressed by our presence. We didn't want to disturb them further, so we quietly and quickly left them behind.

Soon we found our portage to Baby Joe Lake. As a side trip, we took the detour to paddle around Lost Joe Lake. This small lake has only two campsites, but both are well hidden in the trees. Springtime needs an open breezy campsite to blow away the bugs.

A leisurely walk over a portage provides our legs with some exercise and time to study the forest. I love the tangy smell of the pine needles and the musty leaves carpeting the path. Spring's new leaf growth makes the trees such a vibrant green. I searched for all the strange and colourful mushrooms. But this time, we found only wolf and moose scat.

We travelled across Joe Lake, Little Joe Lake, Lost Joe Lake, and Baby Joe Lake. Someone really liked the name, Joe!

One more short portage brought us to Burnt Island Lake. The wind had picked up on this big lake, so we began our hunt for a campsite. Being the first and only ones on this lake, we had many free sites to choose from. We found a site with an accessible shoreline to land our canoe, a good flat spot for our tent, and a smooth rock shoreline with a beautiful view. Maybe all wilderness campsites have good views.

Within two hours of driving and five hours of paddling, portaging, and picture-taking, we encountered a bald eagle, a great blue heron, loons, gulls, and four moose! But only two other humans.

Time for lunch and coffee. And more coffee. The sun came out and warmed us and lured me into the water for a swim. Doug is always much happier just sitting on the sun-warmed rock with his binoculars and watching any canoes passing by.

We set up our tent, bug net, and tarp. You never know when it might rain. Doug must have been entertained or probably frustrated, watching me try and try and try to get that rope over the high branch for the food bag. I could have let him do it, but, you know, I am a little independent. Doug calls it stubborn.

*

Morning arrived with a beautiful sunrise, clear, calm, sunny, and hot. We packed up and set off by 9:30 am. We felt grateful for such calm waters since we had to paddle almost the entire length of this long lake. When we reached the 800-meter portage to Little Otter Slide Lake, we pulled up onto the warm beach and took time for a drink and snack. Usually, the first thing you should do at a portage is to move your stuff out of the way for other paddlers. But we could see no one paddling this morning. Surely no one would be coming across from the other way since we had been the first to cross this lake this season. So, with our canoe and gear scattered about, we sat on a large log in complete peace and quiet.

Suddenly Doug stiffened and whispered. "Shhhh! I hear something in the bush."

With my mouth full of peanuts, I mumbled, "It's probably just a squirrel." But Doug still sat totally stiff as he stared into the forest.

A moose! An enormous chocolate moose slowly emerged from the shadows of the trees. She stopped and stared at us and then at the lake. She came closer, just twenty feet from where Doug sat. Our packs littered her path to the water. She must have thought that humans are so annoying. Slowly she wandered behind Doug and found an alternate way into the water. We watched this wonderful resident of Algonquin Park. So graceful. So silent. We felt overwhelmed with gratitude for the gift of this encounter. We watched until this powerful creature vanished back into the forest. WOW!

Reluctantly leaving this spot, we hoisted our gear and canoe and hiked across the portage. So many fallen trees made this crossing an exercise in gymnastics as we climbed over, ducked low, and bushwhacked around thirteen fallen trees of various sizes. But we loved the wonderful aroma of broken branches, spring sap, pine needles, and cedar boughs. I am pretty sure I heard a saw-whet owl. I tried to pick out the spring calls of all the tiny songbirds.

I have been taking online courses about birds. I never realized how many we have hidden in all our trees. My bird count for this trip included: loons, gulls, cormorants, a bald eagle, a great blue heron, ravens, robins, blue-headed vireo, yellow-rumped warbler, warbling vireo, wood thrush, saw-whet owl, pileated woodpecker, hummingbird, white-throated sparrow, ovenbird, mergansers, black ducks and others that I cannot name, yet.

Finally, back in the water on Little Otter Slide Lake, it didn't take long to find an ideal peninsula campsite. We love all the huge rocks, but sometimes exiting a canoe onto slippery rocks can definitely be another good challenge. Well past noon, I quickly made lunch as Doug set up camp. Hot and sunny, a swim felt so good. We watched only three canoes pass by later that day. A spectacular sunset ended this wonderful day.

*

Morning promised another clear, hot, calm day. By 9:00 am, we packed up the canoe. Why is packing up so tiring?

We retraced our path from the day before. When we reached the portage, Doug discovered that he had forgotten his shoes at our campsite. All he had now was his water shoes, which were slippery and dangerous for crossing any portage. But he did not want to go back. "I will be fine."

166

I felt bad leaving anything behind. But I guess "it will be fine" this one time. I wonder if the next campers at that site would be able to make use of size 12 shoes.

Hot, calm weather made for smooth sailing across the big Burnt Island Lake. We passed by many appealing, vacant sites equipped with counter-like ledges attached between trees and open fire pits areas. But we hoped to get a good location near the west end. We managed to claim a beautiful breezy site. No need for the bug shelter. But we could not find any thunderbox and finally realized it must be buried under one of the tall trees that had obviously come down recently in the wind. Plan B: dig a hole, bury solids, and burn the paper.

We had a huge smooth rock shoreline with a stunning view. Of course, I had to go swimming again.

We had the most unusual tall rock near our fire pit, which looked like a sculpture. Fascinating!

In the night, a noisy and flashy thunderstorm quickly passed over.

*

We must be getting better at this unpleasant job of packing up. The drizzle held off until 8:00 am when we had everything packed, safe, and dry in the canoe and our rain gear on.

169

We headed back the way we had come, travelling over three portages and five lakes. We silently approached the swampy east end of Little Joe Lake in hopes of seeing another moose.

Excitement made it hard not to shout, "Look!" Silently we drifted towards a cow and a massive bull moose grazing hip-deep in the water. We sure didn't get very close this time. Voiceless, we mouthed, "WOW!"

Not wanting to bother this big bull, we soundlessly moved on. As we got far away, we rejoiced loudly at our good fortune. But just as we rounded a point, we startled two other moose. They made a quick escape into the dense wilderness. I could not retrieve my camera quickly enough. They vanished into the forest.

Astonished and amazed. I don't think anyone will believe us when we tell them that we saw nine moose in a four-day canoe trip. But it certainly is true.

Another wonderful trip over, far too quickly.

When we got home, wanting to prove to everyone that we had indeed seen so many moose, we discovered that most of my good close-up pictures had not turned out. I should have learned how to use this new camera better before we left. Most of my photos and videos failed. I am not very tech-savvy. I am SO disappointed that I cannot share my amazement with you.

I hope I get it right next time. Will I ever see another moose again, or have I reached my lifelong quota?

Who cares about the rain and mosquitoes when we are blessed with seeing so many of these magnificent moose? I thank the Creator for all His wonderous creatures, and I pray that we can all better protect and care for them all.

What an unforgettable adventure!

Where are We Going?

Written from Linda Majunke's point of view. Oxtongue River.

Where would Liz be taking me this time? I felt some concerns as she admitted it would be more work than our other canoe trips. What exactly did that mean? I am just happy for this warm, sunny weather to begin our long paddle down the Oxtongue River.

Liz invited me camping many times. First in a cabin, then a yurt, and next in her tiny pop-up trailer. Those times we took a canoe for a day trip and explored many of Algonquin Park's hiking trails.

Finally, I agreed to try canoe camping. My first canoe trip started at Canoe Lake, and we camped on Little Doe Lake for a few days of exploring. For our second adventure, we started at Smoke Lake and stayed on Ragged Lake. On both canoe adventures, we saw serene scenery. Both times we crossed a few lakes and found fabulous campsites. We usually see great blue herons and loons. I have heard the stories of this elusive creature called a moose. But I do not believe that they really exist as I have never, ever seen one. The moose must just be a myth created to lure visitors into Algonquin Park.

Liz explained that since this year we would only be travelling down a river, we had a better chance of seeing moose. I thought it best not to tell her how much I doubted that.

She also explained that this trip might be a little longer than usual. Okay. I can handle that. I compete in Judo tournaments, so I'm fit and do enjoy a challenge, even if it is a little scary.

I parked my car at the huge Canoe Lake lot, and Liz's husband, Doug, drove us to the Tea Lake picnic area. Stepping out of the car, I had to take a deep breath of this fresh, clean air. The aromas of the surrounding trees invigorated me. Glee for this adventure-filled me like a little kid. I saw Liz was energized, too, standing knee-deep in the river, already arranging our gear in the canoe.

At 9:30 am, we left Doug on the shore waving and taking pictures. Liz warned me that finding our campsite might take a while because the river would have many curves, including three short portages. But the current swept us along at a good pace. Massive white pines leaned over us.

Over our first portage, the side of our path dropped sharply down to the noisy Whiskey Rapids. I slipped. Just a little but enough to rip the strap on my shoe. Oh my, ruined. Good thing I packed another pair, but they were hard to find buried amongst the gear in my pack.

We paddled until we reached the walking bridge for the Western Uplands backpacking trail at the Oxtongue picnic area. Here we pulled up on shore and found a table in the shade of a maple tree for a leisurely lunch.

As we travelled on, we searched around every bend in the river and every swampy bay, looking for a moose. But I felt no hope. Moose are just fiction, after all.

The second portage took us around Twin Falls. Two campsites sat right on the portage. Very little privacy here. So strange.

We paddled on, around another bend and another and another. How far would we go? Finally, around 3:00 pm, we found our campsite just past the end of Split Rock Rapids portage. This one was not like any of the lake sites we previously stayed on. It had a sad little fire pit and no sturdy log bench. Many bushes and trees blocked any view of the river and any hope for a breeze. But we certainly could hear the rapids, which looked more like a waterfall to me. At least the newish thunder box proved easy to find.

Setting up the bug net had to be our priority. Of course, being a country kid, Liz didn't find the bugs bad. But they drove me insane. How many bites did I already have from hiking through the trees on all the portages?

Twenty? Forty? Too many. Liz tried to assure me there should not be these many bugs by the end of July. But I don't know if I can believe that either. Are mosquitoes not in the Algonquin wilderness all the time?

Safe in the bug shelter, we relaxed in peace and enjoyed a good cup of tea. Liz couldn't wait to have some of my homemade date squares.

Very close to our site, a smooth, flat, sun-warmed rock in a little calm bay made the shoreline an easy put-in for this end of the portage, as well as a good slip-in for swimming. If we strayed too far, we might never be able to swim back against such a swift current. It felt so good to be in the hot sun, out from under the vampire-infested dense trees.

We found good trees for our hammocks and strung up our big tarps in case of rain. Sooner or later, it will rain. We almost always get some rain.

Then came the fun of finding a tree branch to hang the food bag. I tried so hard not to laugh at Liz's pathetic attempts with her rock bag tied to the rope. Too low. Too far left. Stuck in a different branch altogether. Whacked the tree trunk. Never just right. How many times had she thrown that thing now? Twenty? Forty?

She finally let me try. Well, now I know, it **is** as hard as she makes it look. We do Judo. We throw people, not rocks. A baseball athlete would do better at this than a Judoka.

After a long, hot day of paddling, portaging, and swimming, we wondered why we had seen no other canoeist. None. Content with the privacy and feeling tired, we headed to bed at 9:30 pm.

*

I woke to hear gentle rain hitting my tarp. Warm and cozy, I did not want to get up and face the wet.

I thought I heard Liz up and at it. Maybe? I know there are several small critters that can make more noise than you would think. Birds stir up leaves, looking for bugs. Red squirrels high in the trees drop pinecones. Chipmunks can express a loud warning for their tiny bodies. I did hear a loon in the dark of night.

The thunder box called. Get up.

Liz had been up already. She cut a fallen tree to make it the right size to raise the bug shelter tarp's roof, keep the rain from pooling, and make more room for us since we may be trapped there most of the day.

176

Good thing Liz always brings a few mini-games. Of course, breakfast and lunch gave us some distraction and activity, all safe from bugs and rain within the roofed bug net.

By 4:00 pm, the sun finally freed us from our tiny confines. I needed to stretch, and we could take off the uncomfortable rain gear. Liz really needs new rain gear. It is too big and ugly, for sure.

We wandered along the portage path and took pictures of the rapids.

It is amazing how the rain can suddenly bring out a different aroma from the musty dead leaves. Miraculously mushrooms appear. Liz has a little obsession with these varied and sometimes colourful fungi. She doesn't remember many of their names. But she is trying to teach me all the birds' names that she can distinguish from their pretty songs.

Liz likes to teach, so I encouraged her to let me video her. Maybe these videos can help other new canoe campers. I prompted her with what she could talk about. I like to teach too.

We both felt very surprised to realize that this day we saw no one come by on the portage, no one at all.

Night came quickly, and we crawled into our comfy hammocks.

*

Morning fog certainly made the forest seem eerie, like a lost world. But you never know when you will find surprising beauty.

The warm sun soon dried up the mist—a much-appreciated hot, bright, and leisurely day. We explored a little and wondered where the marked path behind Liz's hammock went, that led deep into the forest. We took more pictures, attempted a few more videos, played some more games and, of course, went swimming.

The relaxation of swimming and floating sure felt good after all the sitting we did the day before. As I crawled out of the water, up the huge smooth rock and sat in the hot sun to dry off, I found a leach. And another. And another. I discovered many tiny leaches between each toe. Pulling them off proved a nasty task. Blood ran all over my feet and down the rock. Liz ran to my rescue with disinfectant and band-aids. But I think she struggled to refrain from laughing at my frantic predicament.

Supper refuelled us. I always look forward to what Liz has packed in the food bag. She somehow managed to make fabulous vegan meals. Such a good variety of flavours and veggies, meatless burgers, soup, stew, pancakes, Bannock, and so many snacks. She plans, packs, and makes all the meals. I do all the clean-ups. I also filter all our water and sterilize it with the magic ultraviolet wand. So easy.

Tomorrow we would be leaving, so we tidied up and packed what we could before bedtime.

*

A familiar sound woke me too early. Rain again. I can endure some rain. But rain makes packing up a pain. Everything had to be kept dry and safe below my hammock all night. Now I had to stay under the tarp to pack everything up. This felt more stressful on my back than being thrown onto Judo mats.

We took time for breakfast before bringing down the bug shelter. We took off at 9:00 am. Thankfully the rain never got worse than a slow, gentle drizzle that soon gave way to a calm, cloudy day.

The never-ending twists of the river took us through a deciduous forest that day. No moose. We passed by the Algonquin Park border. We stopped at a big dock on an uninhabited forest-covered shoreline for a snack and drink. We wondered about the history of this spot as the map indicated a cabin's foundation hid behind us in the trees.

On we paddled with always some slight possibility of a moose encounter. A muskrat scurried up the bank and disappeared into the long grass. Suddenly a beaver directly in front of me slammed his tail on the water. I almost jumped out of the canoe. Liz really laughed out loud this time.

We slowed when passing any small bay or swampy area. Always hoping. Never believing. Never seeing a moose.

It felt like this swift current picked up some speed. We zipped around another bend in the river. Urgently Liz uttered, "STOP."

A cow moose swam directly in front of us with a bull close behind.

They both made an incredibly quick U-turn, hurried up the riverbank and swiftly vanished into the dense forest. Too fast for pictures. But forever in my memory. So close. So huge. So fabulous. WOW! They really do exist! YAY!

We hiked over two little-used portages and paddled further. There were some tense moments reaching the portage entrance as the power of the river wanted to drag us over the rapids. Not doing that.

We paddled on towards our last portage. I wondered if this river would go on and on, forever curving around yet another bend.

Liz assured me we would soon reach our next and final portage at High Falls. There are many High Falls in Algonquin Park, and three you can hike to. One is on the east side of the park on Achray Road, on the Barron River. One is near the southeast corner of the park, on Turner/Basin Road on the Little Bonnechere River, and one is near the very south end of the park on the York River.

We could easily hear the roar of this powerful waterfall. The current wanted to hurl us over the edge. We grabbed onto the bushes along the right shoreline and inched our way to the take-out. Still, here on the shore, the strength of the river tried to pull us.

Safely on shore, we flopped to the ground, shaking. That felt a little too dangerous. We don't mind getting thrown by each other onto a Judo mat. But we do not want to get thrown by a river over a high, rocky cliff.

We grabbed our gear to hike the first half. Slippery from rain, the path felt treacherous down a steep ravine and up the other side, over rocks and roots. We felt damp from the morning's drizzle. The hot afternoon sun came out to bake us in a forest that felt like a sauna.

Thankfully Liz had to stop to catch her breath and pack away her rain gear. The heat tried to force me to remove mine, but I knew the multitude of tiny forest vampires would attack me. Hot or tormented? Hard choice. I went with hot.

We carried on to the first takeout and dropped our heavy loads. This large opening also doubled as a campsite. We sat on a big log for a rest and a needed drink.

On our trek back for the canoe, we had to stop at an excellent lookout spot. These falls are so high and incredibly powerful. So fabulous. Picture time.

Oh boy, we felt weary, but the map assured us that we did not have much further to go. Doug would be meeting us at the Ragged Falls Provincial day-use Park. We did have the option of portaging around these falls and paddling further down the Oxtongue River to end at the Oxtongue Lake Outfitters store. Exhaustion made the choice easy.

As we swept along with the swift current, we finally heard the noise of the falls, so we stuck really close to the left shore and heard Doug call, "Is that you?"

Liz hollered back, "Have you seen anyone else?"

We still could not believe that we had seen no other paddlers for our four days.

I sure appreciated Doug's help as he hauled us out of the grasp of the current. He easily hoisted the canoe and disappeared down the path to the car. But for me, that walk proved to be much longer than I had anticipated. So hot. So tired. So hungry.

3:00 pm. We had paddled and portaged for almost six hours. At sixty-nine, I think Liz may be a little crazy, planning such a long day of strenuous exercise. Do you think so too?

Soon we arrived back at the Canoe Lake outfitter store and restaurant. Liz and I sprinted to the washroom to change into clean clothes. Then I could finally relax at a table by the window overlooking the docks on

Canoe Lake and watch other paddlers leave for a few hours paddle. Or would it be a few days? Their big packs and food barrels would answer that question.

Oh, the smell of fries, coffee, and other good foods intensified my hunger. Soon huge glasses of cold water, big plates with veggie burgers, fries and onion rings, and a salad filled our table. Fabulous!

Liz promised to plan an easier trip for next summer. I felt worn out but triumphant. I now know that moose really do exist.

We parted ways. I headed west and then south. Liz and Doug took off for the east and then north. I think Liz was already planning for our winter excursion of snowshoeing.

More adventures. More fun.

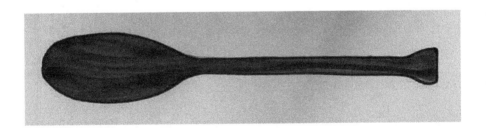

Finally, First Solo

Farm Lake

Some very concerned friends forcefully declared their fears that I must **NOT** go paddling into the wilderness alone.

I tried to assure them that paddling into the wilderness is far less dangerous than driving in the cities. Humans are far more dangerous than any wild animal.

They adamantly insisted that I not go. But I went.

I set off on my first solo canoe trip at the Algonquin Park access point north of Madawaska on Major Lake Rd. I know you will agree that this trip was far too short in time and distance. But excitement filled me so much that nothing could take the huge smile from my face.

At 8:30 am, with my heavy, yellow canoe loaded, Doug watched and worried as I disappeared into the dense fog.

Doug and I had gone this route twice before, so at least he knew where I would be, and I had some idea where to go even though visibility showed me little.

I wound around a couple of bends in the river, but by the time I approached the opening to the little Farm Lake, I still could see next to nothing.

A canoe on the shore told me that someone occupied the first campsite on the lake. The noise from the far end of the lake told me the campsite I had hoped for must be full. I backtracked to an empty site on the river and waited for the fog to lift.

The noise level grew. Hopefully, this large family or group approaching had vacated my hoped-for site. As the sun broke through and dissipated the fog, three canoes loaded with three men each sang and talked loudly as they passed by and waved enthusiastically.

I jumped back into my canoe and enjoyed the return of silence as the warm sun shone brighter.

Nearing the far end of the little Farm Lake, loons greeted me. As I slid onto the beach of the now empty site, I could see a large open area under huge cedar trees with a few level spots for my tent.

With everything set up, I felt confident that I had picked the best spot for the tent and tarp: level, not in a hollow, not near any leaning trees, and the center of the tarp high to keep any rain running away from the tent.

But no rain today. At this site, someone had tied together branches and attached them between two trees to make a ledge. So useful. Someone had used a beer can as a vase for flowers. Cute. But one Algonquin wilderness camping rule is, "Do not bring any cans or glass into the backcountry." At least there were no other beer cans littering the site. I packed this one up to bring out with my plastic garbage.

The hot sun encouraged me to go swimming, although I rarely needed to be encouraged. I love swimming, and I float so effortlessly that it takes no energy at all. Contentedly I could dry off while relaxing on the soft, sandy beach.

The most difficult job for me always proves to be finding a suitable branch for the food bag. But this time, I actually had a few choices.

I took a short paddle around the nearby grassy bay to look for elusive turtles and ducks. I found huge tree roots artfully displayed in the midst of many pretty purple arrowhead flowers and water lilies. Beauty abounds everywhere.

In the middle of the very dark night, two loons had a contest to see whose laughing call was the loudest. The wilderness is not always silent.

*

Morning arrived. After breakfast, I gathered sticks and twigs to store under my tarp as rain clouds moved in. The sky has long fascinated me. The various clouds by day and the multitude of stars by night. What limitless variety of beauty surrounds us! The Creator is amazing!

The clouds thickened, and rain came. I kept dry and comfy under the tarp, napping in the tent. Lazy days are good too. I had books to read, cards to play solitaire, and the sky to watch.

I always hunt around each campsite for garbage to clean up. This site proved nice and clean. But by the foot of a tree, very close to my tent, I found a disintegrating tin can. Since I could not scoop these fragile pieces up, I buried them.

Soon after, I noticed a multitude of bees buzzing about that tree. What had I done?

I realized that I must have closed the opening to their home. Now, what do I do? I sure didn't want angry bees so close to my tent door.

I found a long stick and gently removed the dirt from the opening in the ground at the base of the tree. But of course, they did not understand my well-meant intentions. Sharp burning pain on my foot let me know the extent of their anger. YOW.

A slice of onion held on a bee sting with a band-aid will immediately take the sting away, but I had no stinky onions. I ran for the water and buried my foot in the mud. Ahhhh. Relief. Then I found the aloe vera in my first aid kit, which also helped.

I have no worries about bears but beware the bees! Respect their homes. We are visitors, intruders. Fortunately, since I had fixed my mistake, peace returned.

*

My last day came far too soon. I could have stayed a week if it were not for a worrying husband and friends. I needed to assure them that I had indeed survived.

I leisurely paddled back across Farm Lake and down the river to the take-out beach. Here I hauled my gear and canoe out of the way of the many weekend campers arriving. What an assortment: families with energetic little children, a calm senior couple, groups of boisterous friends with far too much gear, and a few excited dogs.

As I waited for Doug to come and pick me up, I sat snacking under a huge tree and watched the paddlers leave while dense, dark clouds arrived. The rain and thunder chased me into the park office. Lightening flashed fiercely against the dark sky.

Soon the storm passed, leaving a glowing rainbow.

When Doug arrived, I had to show them my pictures. So much beauty fills every moment.

As soon as I got home, I had to share all of this splendour with my fearful friends. But I still may be unable to convince them of the joy of solo canoe camping. They may never understand the rejuvenating peace and the closeness I feel to the Creator in the midst of all this green life that He has wondrously and artistically created.

Then I laid out my Algonquin Park canoe routes map to plan my next trip. So many possibilities.

Come and see!

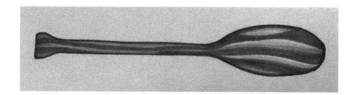

Healing Time

Wendigo Lake to Allan Lake

What a surprise. My youngest daughter, Crystal, announced her desire to go camping with her Dad and me. She struggled with losing her husband, who had just left her. I hoped and prayed that this trip would bring her some peace and joy.

With her work schedule, she could only manage a one-night trip. She has embraced her Cree heritage and explained that she wanted to learn some wilderness skills and be one with nature.

I found a more remote lake that I hoped would not be already all booked, and I managed to reserve a campsite on Allan Lake. We registered at the Brent campground office on the northeast side of Algonquin Park. Then we drove partway down Brent Road and turned onto the tiny trail leading to access #25. By tiny trail, I mean a treacherous path for anything other than an ATV. I drove our little car with our two canoes perched on our small utility trailer, travelling at four kph. Doug anxiously begged, "Slow down!"

After much bouncing and jerking, we finally arrived at Wendigo Lake. Wendigo is the Algonquin people's name for a carnivorous monster who eats people. He must live in the form of this trail as it surely tried to devour us.

Finally, we found the parking lot, and we could stop holding our breath. By parking lot, I mean a very small, sloped, and rocky area, totally rammed full of cars, trailers, and big pick-ups. But Doug has a talent for finding or making a spot when there is none. Our car had to park on the edge of the opening, jammed in the long grass against the trees.

No worries, my excitement could never be dimmed. We headed south on Wendigo Lake, hugging the west shore. This was my first trip with my new blue solo canoe, Serenity. Crystal and her Dad took their time, so I would not fall far behind. She is a strong paddler but loves taking selfies that helped slow them. My narrow canoe slid easily on the water, and I had no trouble keeping up. Initially, it felt quite tippy, but I quickly became comfortable and felt at ease.

We made it to our only portage. Short and easy, which made it a good introduction for my girl. As we entered Allan Lake, the wind picked up. How would my little canoe do now? No worries. With my big pack rammed in the bow, I felt very stable and confident.

We headed straight for the center island about halfway down the lake. I hoped that the campsite would be vacant. We had met only two other paddlers on the portage, but soon left them far behind. We maneuvered around the rocky island and, on the south shore, found a sandy, little beach from which we could see the campsite sign and no campers. Yay. We got it. What a beautiful site. Tall red pines made a soft carpet of aromatic pine needles on most of this long high island. The far end held denser, shorter trees, thankfully hiding the thunderbox.

We ran around like little kids let out for recess, exploring our island. I made coffee and lunch as the other two set up the tents. Time to relax and enjoy our surroundings. What a beautiful panoramic view of the entire lake. Loons called a welcome.

We heard a panicky scream from Crystal inside her tent. Poor girl saw a bug. We reminded her of her Native roots and her desire to be one with nature. She was not impressed with my lack of sympathy, but we all giggled anyway.

Crystal couldn't wait to hang up the tiny hammock and dig out her book. Doug's favourite camping toy, or I should say, the only toy he is allowed to bring is binoculars. He studies the far shorelines for any signs of life. Hoping to see a moose. A bear may scare him.

If other paddlers come close, he loves to ask how far they are going. How long? Where are they from? Most are friendly but don't slow their pace for too long as they are eager to find their campsite.

Happy campers. Happy to be free. Happy to be here. Happy for a canoeing adventure. So thankful for this healing time for my daughter to be surrounded and rejuvenated by all this living, green wilderness. Embarrassed by God's healing, powerful love.

I had to go swimming. I always must go swimming. This was my last chance this season for an Algonquin swim. This summer, I swam in five different Algonquin lakes.

With the chance of rain, we set up the tarp, always with the goal of being able to play cards nice and dry. Finding a nice flat surface to place the cards always poses a challenge. Sitting around this flat spot can take some invention. Leaning against a tree perched on a life jacket can be comfortable for a while, but inevitably the pine needles cause the life jacket to slide. And soon, the nice posture becomes a slouch. Not so easy to play games, then. Okay, let's just have a nap.

The afternoon soon became supper time. Later we roasted marshmallows. Silly daughter had to ask Dad to tell the Tom Thomson story again. How many times have I heard it now? I know all the "who done it" theories of this murder mystery.

Doug can be quite entertaining and even ridiculous. How can he think so fast to be so silly? My Mama's heart glowed to hear Crystal laugh loudly, like a carefree child.

We listened to the loons serenade us to sleep. Peace and calm. I heard the intriguing call of an owl in the middle of the dark night. I heard it multiple times and from different locations. Maybe he was flying around the lake? Maybe two called to each other? Maybe he was a long-eared owl?

I always sleep well when camping, and so did Crystal, despite her fears of bugs and the dark.

*

The morning sky showed no signs of the sun. After breakfast and a leisurely coffee, we headed off to the portage at the south end of Allen Lake. We left our canoes and ran over the short trail to look at North Depot Lake. The winding creek that leads to the lake had very bushy banks making it impossible to follow the shoreline far enough to have a good view of this narrow lake. Then the rain began, and we hid under tall, dense cedar trees to keep dry.

No worries. We had no schedule, no hurry to do anything, and we could just enjoy the peace and quiet.

The rain turned to a soft mist as we paddled back to our campsite for lunch. Too soon, our time here drew to an end. We slowly packed up and loaded our canoes. The drizzle returned, so we all put on our rain gear for our return paddle to the car.

As I carefully stepped into my narrow, loaded canoe, I lost my balance and fell entirely into the lake. The rain gear protects you from rain but will not keep you dry if you swim. End up!

After a good laugh, we could finally take off. No worries. The warmth of the day prevented any chills even though I sat soaked. I didn't care. I love canoe camping, no matter what silly slip-ups occur.

While crossing the lake, we constantly watched the shoreline. Doug felt sure that every dark rock must be a bear. But no. We saw no bear. We did manage to spy a great blue heron and watched in awe as he gracefully flew away. Wow.

Beauty surprises me everywhere I look. Each tree, each leaf, each flower and each petal, each creature and each person is so totally, marvellously unique. I realize God's great love for all His creation in His amazing imagination and detailed artistry.

The drizzle quit before our paddling ended. We loaded up the canoes and gear. We took turns hiding in the bushes to change into clean, dry clothes, since we would be stopping for dinner on the three-hour drive back home.

What a tremendous blessing to spend such a special time with our adventurous daughter. The time was far too short. Mamas always find that the time with grown kids is far too short. This Mama thanks God every day for the blessing of my five grown children.

Please, let's do it again.

Serenity

Solo, Lake Magnetawan to Mubwayaka Lake

The drizzle forced me to wear all my rain gear, but I felt sunny inside. I had a huge smile while paddling away from the dock at the access point on Lake Magnetawan. I eagerly took off on my first solo trip with my new solo Swift canoe, "Serenity." I had been working towards this for years. Don't ask how many years, or you will surely ask, "What took you so long?"

I didn't plan a long or strenuous trip. I have some idea of my limited abilities. Still smiling, I flew over the easy portage and sailed across Hambone Lake.

Another short portage brought me to Ralph Bice Lake. Even though I had only met one other paddler so far, I knew that in this early part of August, Algonquin Park could be very full. Would I need to travel to the far end of this bigger lake to find an empty campsite?

As I paddled the first narrow part of the lake, I felt the wind grow. By the time I reached the large open area, the wind and waves bashed into me. I had never paddled my slim Serenity in much wind. I wondered if I made any headway at all as I slowly fought my way past occupied campsites. Thirst demanded I pause to grab a drink, but the wind threatened to slam me against the rocky shore. So, I pushed on past more busy campsites. I kept paddling, struggling against the growing wind. But my heavy packs helped me to stay stable through the turbulence.

Finally, I found an empty site. I dragged my gear and canoe ashore and stood watching the whitecaps zing by. I made it with Serenity and answered prayers. I know God can calm the winds and waves, but He knows I enjoy a good challenge.

Although I wanted lunch and coffee but first the tarp needed to go up. The drizzle could quickly turn to a soaking rain. But I continued to smile.

I found an excellent place for my hammock. This would be my second trip with my hammock, and I debated the pros and cons of a tent versus a hammock for a solo trip. The hammock won. I find it so cozy. I usually toss and turn and found that I can sleep in more positions in a hammock than my back will allow on a flat bed.

I enjoy the solitude. But I can't say it was quiet, with such a strong wind swaying the tall trees and waves smashing onto the rocky shore.

No real rain fell, so I could enjoy my campsite, lunch, and coffee. And another coffee. I explored, gathered firewood, and fell into bed soon after supper.

*

The morning brought clouds again. I packed up and headed out to find the portage to David Lake. Not an easy take-out on that steep bank.

A short quick crossing of David Lake brought me to the tiny portage to Mubwayaka Lake. By then, the wind had grown, and drizzle threatened again. I usually like to paddle for about fifteen minutes on one side and then switch to keep my muscles symmetrical. But the wind would only allow me to paddle on one side. No need to do the 'J stroke' because I had to paddle hard and fast on the left side to keep from being turned left, and I needed to head right. Thankfully I didn't have far to go. I enjoyed the short, hard workout.

What a big, beautiful site I found. Lots of level spots for tents, although a hammock doesn't need a level spot. I had many good trees to choose from.

Moose evidently like this site as well, as I found many piles of scat.

The abundance of recent rain produced many mushrooms, which I find fascinating—so many varieties of fungus, so many shapes, colours, and textures. Even though I have been studying five thousand kinds of fungi in Ontario, it can be very difficult to distinguish some of the healthy from the deadly.

I also find owls fascinating. My fuzzy buddy Finn joined me so I could take a series of "Find Finn" photos just for fun.

210

In the morning, I packed up and had a very short trip back to David Lake, where I found the island site vacant. What fun. I had lots of time to set up, explore, take pictures, read, and enjoy the peace. There are only two campsites on Mubwayaka Lake and David Lake, and no one occupied these other sites.

So many people ask if I am ever scared out there all alone. My response is a quick, "Never!"

Then they insistently add, "But what about…" and list all the things I guess they fear. But again, I immediately reply, "Never."

But I am careful. I wear a whistle at all times. No man nor beast wants to stick around a blasting whistle.

I always tie my food bag off a high branch, which I have to say is the most challenging job of wilderness camping. It can be quite a task to find a suitable branch. First, I must find a rock that is not too heavy for me to throw but heavy enough to pull the rope. I drop the rock into an old sock that I can tie to the long rope. Then I hunt for the right branch, hopefully more than thirty meters from my hammock. The branch must be strong enough to hold the weight of the food and long enough so that the food bag hangs one meter away from the tree trunk and at least four meters off the ground.

Solo camping means no one witnesses my multiple attempts to throw that rope over the only suitable branch in my area. You would not believe how my rock bag can unpredictably fly in the wrong direction or get snagged in the wrong branch, and I yank and tug and jerk only to retrieve the rope alone. Already this summer, I have had to abandon a couple of rock bags irretrievably stuck high in the trees. Then I must dig out another old sock from my gear and hunt for another suitable rock to attach to my rope and try again, and again, and again. Wishing my baseball-playing son could help. I have to laugh at just how ridiculous my pitches must look. At least my arm is never sore the next day.

The year before, I attended a workshop on wilderness camping which informed me that the two most likely injuries are burns and ankle injuries. I bring a well-supplied first aid kit. I make sure my stove is level and stable, and the pot handle is secure. I don't hurry over portages but watch every step over the tricky rocks, roots, and slippery mud.

This island campsite had two huge boulders in the center with trees growing out of the tops. How does that happen?

The fire pit had been built up high and had good flat rocks for placing my tiny stove, and I didn't have to fear spilling my full cup of hot coffee. And the larger flat rocks made good seats. Bonus.

Lots of possible level spots available here to pitch a tent and well-spaced trees to hang a tarp. I decided to experiment and put my hammock on the ground this time, as there seemed to be no rain in the forecast. I pegged it down so it wouldn't slide anywhere and attached the bug net to the tarp. This gave me a little more space but did not feel quite as cozy.

The next day, I crossed the longer portage back to Ralph Bice Lake. With so much mud to maneuver around, I got a good workout on the portage. Then I had a very short paddle to the vacant site on another island.

I know you may see this canoe trip on the Algonquin canoe routes map and conclude that my daily treks looked far too short. Please don't judge me too harshly or think me wimpy. I have my black belt in Judo, and my instructor declared, "Wimps don't get their black belts."

But since this was my first real travelling solo canoe trip and I was in my late sixties, I had to face the reality of my limitations. Sometimes reality stinks.

Another reality is that Ralph Bice is a good-sized lake and probably almost full. Who could have guessed that I would not have had to travel

213

most of the lake to find an empty site? How could I be so fortunate that this site, which probably had the best view, would be vacant?

This campsite had a smooth take-out on a huge, sun-warmed rock. I hauled all my gear up the hill and wandered around the big open, sloped area, searching for a good spot to hang my hammock. On this sunny day, I didn't need to hurry to get the tarp up.

But where did they hide the thunderbox? Fortunately, a tiny yellow sign gave me a hint, and I followed the narrow path through the bush, winding far up the hill. It would be far too far if you must go in a hurry. Oh, my!

Lunchtime. Swim time. I relaxed and enjoyed the view of the big lake. Binoculars helped to see the rocky shore, cliffs, and a few campsites on the far side of the lake.

Noisy chattering disturbed the silence. Someone, hidden from my view by the trees, approached close along my island shore. Slowly and silently, I crept towards the rocky edge to see who would appear. Expecting one or two canoes with young, excited children, I sat waiting. A family of twenty-two common merganser ducks surprised me. What could they be talking about?

I think they were also startled to see me and probably disappointed that I occupied this sun-warmed, rocky shore. They moved out from shore, and as if one of them gave a signal, they all dove under the water in unison.

I do a lot of paddling and camping in Ontario's wilderness and rarely see any ducks. Common mergansers are the most common. There are so many other kinds, yet scarcely seen. Some are divers, like loons and this big family. Some are dippers, like the mallard and Canada goose. Some large, some tiny, all uniquely beautiful. My favourite is the small, hooded merganser. My husband likes the white bufflehead. They each have their own behaviours, characteristics, and beauty. All are so timid and rarely seen. Where have all the ducks gone?

This year I scarcely saw any turtles either. Where have they gone? I have heard that most of our Ontario turtles are endangered. So sad. We need to see all life, all our fellow creatures, as beautiful and needing our compassion and protection, not destruction.

Usually, campsites have many trees suitable for hanging a tarp or hammock and level land for tents. This one, however, did not. The trees stood too close or too far on this sloped site for my hammock. Luckily, I had found some good, abandoned rope at my first campsite. I put this supply of extra rope to good use here for the tarp. One tree I needed to hang the tarp from stood too far from the rest. The hammock had to be placed under it, on the ground this time, on the only level spot available.

But what an amazing view. Laying in a hammock gives you a better view and allows you to be closer to the beauty of nature.

*

I didn't want to get up the next morning. I just lay there and enjoyed the spectacular sunrise. I felt in no hurry to pack up and leave. But the photographer in me forced me to get up, find my camera and capture the beauty for you.

I certainly took my time to enjoy every fleeting moment of my last day. I enjoyed a wind-free return across Ralph Bice Lake to the easy portage back to Hambone Lake, which I crossed to my last portage. This being Saturday showed me how difficult a portage could be with so many paddlers arriving. A traffic jam in Algonquin Park causes no stress. Everyone proved to be courteous as they excitedly began their journey. I sat with my gear well out of the way, watching the great variety of campers off-load their gear and hike over the portage. What fun entertainment.

Two slim and trim young Park Rangers arrived. With all the extra gear they had to carry, I could tell they would be replacing some thunder boxes, and I had to thank them for the hard work they had ahead of them. Good job, boys!

As I reached the end of my trip at Lake Magnetawan, I met a friendly lady, maybe close to my age, who told me that she had been solo canoe camping for many years. Decades even. What an inspiration. She quickly and gently gave tips to two young Irish couples who loaded up their canoes for their very first wilderness trip. I would love to thank this lady for her inspiration and for sharing her joy with others.

I wish I could have later asked these two couples how they enjoyed their time in Canada's beautiful Algonquin Park. In rain and wind or sun and calm, you will see a big smile on my face the whole time.

I wish I could thank the late Esther Keyser, the first female canoeing guide in Algonquin Park, whose autobiography, *Paddle My Own Canoe*, sparked my passion for canoe camping. And, of course, a huge thanks to Kevin Callan for all his helpful hints, for sharing his enthusiasm for canoeing into the wilderness, for his many informative books and oh-so-entertaining videos, and for sharing his enthusiasm for canoeing in the wilderness.

Is This Really the River?

Solo, North River to Merganser Lake.

I stopped to get my permit at the Brent office near highway 17. Then we continued to drive down that long gravel road to hunt for my access point. This road passes by a hiking trail that leads to a tall look-out tower from which you can barely make out the Brent crater. Eons ago, a meteor slammed into our planet, causing massive devastation. Hard to imagine now that the forest hides most of the evidence. Makes me wonder when and where another meteor could fall.

We found the small parking lot, which held only one car at this access point, maybe halfway down the gravel road to the Brent campground. I knew I would not meet many campers. Doug felt very hesitant about leaving me. He did not think I would be able to get through the narrow North River. This surely did not look like a river, a creek, maybe.

The first half of my morning's travel meandered on a very narrow overgrown creek, which proved not wide enough even to put my paddle in, and I had to propel myself along by pulling on the branches.

Don't be discouraged by what may lie ahead. One paddle stroke at a time. You can do it. Maybe in life, too, one step at a time.

I started my trip in the drizzle again. Of course, I took my time. No need to race anyone for a campsite.

The river widened slightly just in front of three beaver dams, which I easily dragged my loaded canoe over.

The last part of this endlessly winding river wandered through a huge, soggy bog.

Finally, it opened up to a small lake where curious otters greeted me. At the far end, where this North Lake narrowed, I found the short easy portage to Merganser Lake. As I made my second trip across the portage, a friendly solo kayaker landed. He had with him a saw and quickly removed the tree lying across our path. I headed out first and followed the west shore to hunt for a campsite.

The tarp goes up first when rain threatens. Then I had to climb uphill over many fallen trees to find the disintegrating thunderbox. I cleared away a few of these long trees to make the path less hazardous.

I relished my coffee and lunch while enjoying the pretty view, surrounded by God's living beauty. Maybe here, on a solo trip into the wilderness, is the best place to truly be still and draw closer to the Creator.

The sun came out, and the day turned warm and beautiful. Time for a swim. A couple of explorers camped on North Lake paddled by. Loons and a flicker kept me company.

*

The next day my little Swift canoe, Serenity and I explored this pretty little lake. Around the narrow rocky island, I hunted for the portage heading south. I took a hike over this longer low maintenance portage, but drizzle returned, which cut my exploring short and convinced me to return to my campsite.

Thankfully, I had the luxury of a good tiny camping chair to sit comfortably. I finished a book on prayer and started one about God's promises. I remembered that God sometimes says, "Peace. Be still". Trust Him. Listen for His voice. I love the stillness and peace of solo camping. No one in sight. Surrounded not by walls and steel and pavement but only by green life, a few birds and tiny, fuzzy creatures. Maybe this is a little glimpse of Eden.

The sun returned on this lazy day to energize me. The campfire pit looked as shabby as the thunderbox, so I fortified the pit with more stones. I found a few big flat ones to place as a level table for my tiny propane stove and to place my cup. Pouring hot water into a mug only to have it spill can be frustrating, if not dangerous. Some level spots surely help.

For fire starters, I gathered some clumps of dried moss, pinecones, and small twigs. I broke larger branches off the fallen, dead trees, karate kicked them into shorter pieces and piled them beside the first collection, about two metres away from the fire pit. This would surely be too much for me, but the golden rule of camping is, "Leave the campsite better than you find it."

The solo camper I met on the portage had left the path better than he found it. Maybe we could all work to leave our campsite, our neighbourhood, and our world better than we first find it.

What a fun blessing to arrive at a clean and well-supplied campsite after paddling and portaging for hours.

Sleeping in my hammock is so cozy, and I love being able to see all around and watch the sun set and rise. But the night became so chilly that I had to get up and put on all the clothes I had brought. All layered up; I slept warm and well.

*

My hammock hung fairly close to the lake. At first light on my last day, I heard a sound exactly like a huge rock thrown into the water very near me. I guess this loud noise in the early dawn would have undoubtedly scared many, but I immediately knew it could only be a beaver smacking his big flat tail on the water's surface. He must have caught my scent and attempted to warn me to stay away from him or other beavers to stay away from me, maybe?

I took time for a leisurely breakfast, then reluctantly packed everything except my rain gear. I had to wear it because the drizzle began just as I loaded Serenity and left this lovely retreat.

This had been planned as a five-day trip but threatened thunderstorms cut it short. What a disappointment to have to shorten my trip.

I don't mind the rain. But thunderstorms are not safe for paddling. Thankfully it only rained intermittently, and no wind challenged me.

I met another friendly solo camper, fishing on North Lake, who said he would be cutting his stay short as well because of the forecasted thunderstorms and would soon follow me up the river. I had not heard nor seen any sign of storms…yet. This winding river afforded absolutely no place to get onto firm land if any lightning arrived. Only the three beaver

225

dams stood solid but were far too exposed. The first twenty minutes travelled through swampy bog. The last half hour, the shore was totally blocked by the low, thick bushes and branches. But I could see that many branches had been cut, making the narrow passageway a little easier to navigate. The solo kayak camper with the saw, had returned yesterday and must have taken much time making this route easier for the rest of us.

The drizzle remained constant. I do not have any fancy or expensive waterproof footgear, so I sat in the chilly drizzle with raincoat and rain pants but bare feet to be ready for the beaver dam crossings.

Just as I began to wonder, "Are we there yet?" I emerged from the dense branches to the narrow muddy take out. Doug rushed down to the shore to greet me. We hurriedly loaded everything into and onto the car as the other solo canoer arrived. Even though I felt cheated by having to shorten my trip, I sure felt happy to see Doug, change into clean clothes and warm my feet.

Of course, the drive home always includes the treat of a veggie burger and fries. And hot coffee. And ideas for my next trip.

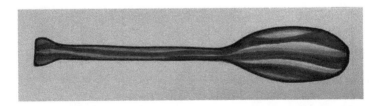

Stuck in the Muck
Tim River

Have you heard the expression "Best laid plans"? I thought this well-planned trip would be easy.

I booked this trip five months in advance. Since this route warns of possible low water levels, I chose June, hoping for spring's higher water.

I would be exploring new territory for my first solo canoe trip this summer. Anticipation woke me up before the alarm, which was set for 4:00 am. After a four-hour drive, I arrived at access point # 2, Tim River, near the northwest corner of Algonquin Park. The dense clouds, drizzle, and a chilly 8 degrees Celsius may have darkened some campers' spirits, but I shone with excitement. By 9:00 am, I sat in my loaded canoe, wearing my ugly rain gear again. This day would be easy.

Slowly I paddled the constantly curving Tim River through the swampy bog. The beauty of spring flowers, colours, and fragrances surrounded me—pretty purple irises, sweet gale's tiny flowers and many

227

others that I could not name. I found the unusual, unique star flowers of the pitcher plants. Is this the only carnivorous plant in Canada? The pitcher-shaped leaves fill with water and a secretion which drowns and ingests bugs. I had never seen their flowers before. What treasures do we miss everywhere if we do not take the time?

Picture time. So quiet. So peaceful. No other humans. Many birds sang and flittered about in this busy breeding season. A Kingbird perched in her nest. She tried to sink low into the nest to hide. But she would not leave her eggs. The Red-winged blackbirds are extremely territorial and will attack anyone invading their territory, including hawks, eagles, and even humans. Thankfully I didn't need a hard hat this time.

I saw no moose on this stretch to Tim Lake, even though others assured me, "If you want to see moose, you paddle the Tim River."

Tim River grew wider and opened into Tim Lake. With no portages to do this day, I had an easy trip to my first campsite at the far southeast end of the little lake.

The sun came out, warming the day. I took my time setting up my hammock and tarp, relaxed in the welcomed sun, enjoyed lunch, and relished my hot coffee. With lots of time to explore, I found a massive maple with the best branch ever to hang my food bag. While hunting for campfire wood, I found the remains of a big cabin, a root cellar and possibly a well. Had this been a logging camp? Maybe there are more buildings hidden deeper in the forest.

I collected much firewood but didn't use it. I used my tiny camp stove for cooking. But I almost always collect wood for the next campers.

My cozy hammock called me to bed just at sunset. Sleep comes easily, quickly, and soundly with such peace and quiet. The calm silence was suddenly shattered by a boisterous outburst of two loons very close, competing to see who could be the loudest.

*

The night had been chilly, but I packed appropriately and felt warm and comfy. Hopefully, the bright morning sun would bring the temperature closer to normal for this late in June. I took time for breakfast and tea before packing up. Leaving at 9:00 am, I headed out on what I thought would be an easy three-hour paddle across this end of Tim Lake and then down the meandering Tim River to Rosebury Lake.

I met the first beaver dam as Tim Lake narrowed into a large swampy bay. There, as promised, stood a massive, glistening, chocolate-brown bull moose. I silently paddled closer, hidden behind little knolls of tall grass and sweet gale bushes. I got a few good photos before he headed toward the forest.

Not daring to disturb him in his home, I headed towards the short portage around an old dam.

Here the river narrowed. A warning on the map indicated that this part of the river could be difficult at low water levels. That is why I booked this trip for June, hoping the spring water levels would still be high enough for a trouble-free paddle. But who could have predicted that this would be an extremely dry spring?

I anticipated the fun challenge of some beaver dams to slide or climb over. But I lost count after ten.

After each dam, the river level lowered until there seemed to be only a trickle over the long, lime-green grasses. I hoped that I would be able to slide easily over this area since I travelled light in my little solo canoe 'Serenity.'

No, I could not. I rammed my paddle into the two inches of water and pushed. But the paddle sunk two feet into the black, unbearably putrid muck. Pulling out the paddle moved me backwards. That would not work well. I grabbed my spare paddle and pushed both paddles in on either side. I pushed hard, which moved me only four inches forward. Yanking the paddles out of the sinking mud pulled me two inches back. So, I stood up and tried to see downstream to get some hint of how far I would have to travel like this.

I debated returning to Tim Lake. One park rule says, "You must camp on the lake you booked to be on." But in bug season, there are not many canoe campers out here, and certainly, not all the sites would be reserved.

How could I continue, on this mud path, with such painfully slow progress?

Just then, I saw someone walking towards me through the bog. How did he find any solid ground through all the sweet gale bushes? I saw the long rope he had attached to his canoe where his partner slowly inched her way up the river towards me. Despite how worn out they appeared, they sounded cheerful. I asked how far this shallow area stretched. She assured me that with my solo canoe and little gear I should not have as much difficulty as they had. I informed them they only had a short distance before the river deepened.

For a long stretch, I could not paddle but pushed hard with very slow progress. This turned my three-hour leisurely paddle into a six-hour struggle. Fifty deerflies tormented me until twenty dragonflies came to my rescue.

Endless twists almost convinced me that this river struggle would never end. Finally, I could see Rosebury Lake. Finally, I could actually paddle again out into the open water. Exhaustion forced me to rest. I considered the map and looked around to determine which campsite to head for. The north end of the lake had a long beach, and my binoculars let me know this campsite was vacant.

What a relief to pull up on shore, stretch my legs and set up camp. I found the perfect spot on this little peninsula to hang my hammock with a wonderful view of the entire lake. I had an open breezy, bug-free campfire pit with good log benches. In one direction, a short trail led to the thunderbox; on the other side of the site, another narrow path led to the long, sun-warmed beach.

I planned to use this beach the next day as I would stay here for two nights. My comfy hammock called me to bed far too early.

*

The morning sun gave me hope for a nice hot day. Yesterday's struggle down the river caused painfully sore muscles in my arms and chest. I almost felt relieved when the wind arrived, creating monster waves that nixed my plans to paddle around and explore the lake this day.

The wind grew and intensified. The wild gusts threatened to hurl anything not anchored far into the forest. I had to fight to keep my stove's wind barrier from flying away.

I took a leisurely stroll down the long beach in the bright sun hoping for a calm spot in the warm sun to relax and rejuvenate. But the enormous white-capped waves crashed onto the shore, and the incessant wind stole the sun's warmth. In the sand, I found evidence of someone else who had previously strolled here, the giant footprints of a moose.

Near the centre of the beach, I met two families of geese with young goslings. Of course, they did not appreciate my intrusion and leapt into the waves hoping to get away from me. But the wind and waves barred their escape. No matter how hard they tried, they could only get ten feet from shore. To restore their peace, I quickly returned up the path through the trees back to my camp.

I collected firewood but made no fire. The crazy wind made that too dangerous. The tarp over my hammock flapped violently in its attempt to break free and fly far, far away. One rope broke, tearing the tarp. I realized that I needed to find a more secluded spot deeper into the forest, or I may have no tarp left. What a job! I had to untie and take down the tarp without the wild wind whipping it away. Finding a calmer spot proved difficult. The trees had to be a good space apart, far away from dead or leaning trees. Then came the fight with the gusts to retie all the ropes. I hoped and prayed that my tarp would survive.

While making lunch, I sat close to my tiny stove. I brought a comfy chair this time. Whenever I got up from the chair, I rammed it under the log bench to keep the wind from hurling it far away.

Except for one time I wanted to quickly get something out of a bag by my hammock.

Nope. When I turned around, my chair appeared to have blown right onto the stove's flames. Instinctively I bolted over the short distance.

Never run on uneven ground littered with rocks and roots.

What a shock when I fell. I smacked my head hard. Ouch. That left a big nasty bump. I must have thrown my back out too. Many sore muscles complained about the previous day's struggle. Ouch. I sure didn't feel like moving much, and I dreaded tomorrow's return trip up that muddy path.

A cold washcloth dipped in the chilly water helped to bring down the welt on my forehead, and aspirin helped my aches and pains.

I must admit that I do love my vegan camp meals. Relaxed in my rescued and undamaged chair, I could enjoy my huge meals and hope they would help heal my injuries and rejuvenate me for the next day's challenge.

Soon my bed called to me. The insane wind still threatened to rip away my tarp. No silence in this night, but still, I slept well and long.

*

Cloudy dawn woke me to a new world, calm and quiet, with a musty odour created by the dismal, damp drizzle of the night.

I leisurely packed up, not because I had lots of time but because I ached everywhere. Luckily the lump on my forehead had shrunk even though it felt very sore to the touch.

I headed back up the dreaded dry Tim River. I repositioned my gear, hoping it would set me higher in the water, but the trip still took six hours of pushing, pushing, pushing up the mucky trickle and pulling and hauling over the ten beaver dams.

Fifty deer flies buzzed around my head and tortured each hand. But I had no energy to fight with them. The drizzle must have chased away all the dragonflies.

Finally, I reached the short portage. As I hauled my big pack up the wet, slippery, steep hill, I met five guys with two canoes coming toward me. I warned them of the shallow creek, but I don't think they believed me. They would soon realize the truth with great frustration.

Watching them push off, I wished them luck. I tried to hoist my light canoe for my last trip across to deeper water. But my chest and arm muscles cried in agony, and my back groaned, making my attempt awkward and agonizing.

I didn't have far to go now. I paddled slowly through the large swampy area and searched for the moose in vain. Suddenly the silence shattered with what must have been one hundred bullfrogs all singing in amazing harmony. The choir grew louder until it sounded like an army hunting me down, chasing me out of their territory. I had to keep looking back. Surely, they sounded right behind me in full pursuit.

As I rounded a bend into the narrow opening to Tim Lake, I could see the nearest campsite. The drizzle turned to rain. My muscles cried in pain.

I flung my gear out of the canoe and dragged it up the bank. Two perfect trees for my hammock had a good view and were not far from the thunder box.

It would be a wet evening. As quickly as my aching muscles allowed, I had my tarp up and all my gear protected under it. I collapsed into my chair and felt like crying. Aspirin helped. I never thought it possible, but agony replaced my appetite with nausea. So, I sat, just listening to the persistent rain. At least no wind threw the wet under my tarp, and I could stay dry and warm. There would be no sitting by a toasty fire this evening. Finally, hunger returned, and I could make my yummy dinner and restore some energy. I crawled into my bed extra early, listening to the continuous rain and slept well.

*

Another dark wet morning woke me, and I had to wear my awkward rain gear again. The pain forced me to move slowly, and I hoped oatmeal and tea would warm and energize me.

I had struggled along the extremely shallow river, survived a wild wind, a painful fall, and persevered despite aching muscles. God is my ever-present help in trouble. Never give up. Never surrender.

Working in the confined area under the tarp, I packed everything up in agony. Pushing off from the bank, I so wished I could have enjoyed this picturesque peninsula overlooking half of Tim Lake.

Paddling around the big central island, a loon surprised me. He popped up right beside me and performed a dazzling dance. What cheerful fun. This put a smile back on my face all the while I paddled to the end of the lake and continued up the twists and turns of the Tim River.

Finally, the rain ended, and the sky lightened. I could see the bridge and the parking lot. Doug waited but was not alone on the riverbank. An energetic couple loaded up their canoe to begin their adventure. Doug pulled my damp mess up onto the muddy shore.

Doug had told this friendly young couple that he was waiting for me to return from my five-day solo trip. They wanted to have a picture with me as they explained that I inspired them. I felt famous, but I wondered how I must look, muddy and messy.

Their planned trip would take them much further and longer than my trip. They inspired me.

I threw all my soggy gear in the trunk as Doug loaded my canoe on top of the car. As soon as I flopped into the car, I pulled down the visor for the mirror so I could comb my dishevelled hair. Oh crap! An ugly bruise tried to hide behind my bangs.

The long, curving dirt road took us out of the wilderness and back toward civilization and Huntsville. I had to tell my caring husband the story of the gruesome struggle on the muddy river. I had to admit the truth of the map's warning of the Tim River's difficult low water levels. I had to explain my colourful forehead. Oh boy, will he let me go on another solo canoe trip? He surely had better, as I already had paid for two more.

I described all the beautiful flowers I had seen, the ruins of the cabin hidden in the forest, the long sandy beach with the fuzzy goslings, the army of hundreds of bullfrogs and the dancing loon. Of course, I had to tell the story of paddling through the large swampy area, silently drifting to hide behind sweet gale bushes, to take pictures of the massive bull moose. This confirms what is said about this area, "If you want to see moose, travel the Tim River."

Despite the difficult challenge and injuries, this proved to be another phenomenal experience. I can't wait for the next one!

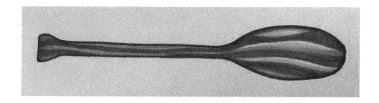

What are the Odds?
Aura Lee Lake

I wonder if everyone feels anxious when heading out on the notoriously windy, long Cedar Lake. This morning I just had drizzle to contend with. What are the odds that I would have drizzle to begin my trip yet again?

The dark clouds tried to dampen my spirits. But no way would that succeed. At 8:30 am, Doug shoved me off the beach at the Brent Campground on Cedar Lake.

Only one other canoe headed out, but they travelled south, and I went north.

A large cottage sits high on an island near the north end of Cedar Lake. Another smaller island has a campsite with a tall stone fireplace, the remnants of a cabin.

At the top end of Cedar Lake, I paddled through a narrow passageway over an extremely shallow rocky ridge that has scraped the paint off many canoes. I found an area that my light Serenity could pass over unscathed. After the short paddle across Little Cedar Lake, I found the narrow river that led to the smaller Aura Lee Lake. This river travels under the bridge for the train that used to run along the east side and across the top of

Algonquin Park. Hidden in the forest are the remains of many tiny towns. This area has much rich history of the first settlers to this part of Canada.

As I paddled under this old cement bridge, the noise of two noisy motorboats assaulted my senses. I could not imagine how they got to Aura Lee Lake when even a canoe had difficulty over the shallow rock ledge. There are no motorboats allowed on most of Algonquin's interior lakes.

Thus far, I had not encountered any other paddlers. A gentle dog greeted me at the easy portage to Laurel Lake. As I pulled onto the rocky shore, a friendly couple loaded their canoe. They voiced their shock at hearing the noisy motorboats zipping up and down the tiny Aura Lee Lake.

Once on Laurel Lake, I checked the map to decide where to camp. Surrounded by hills, this pretty lake has only a few campsites, with one perched high on a small island. I had my choice since most spots looked vacant, and I chose a point with a panoramic view. Don't all Algonquin sites have a wonderful view? Most are so secluded and quiet. You may see other paddlers far out on the lake but rarely hear anyone. Later in the day, a family arrived at a campsite which I could only see with my binoculars. But I could hear the children's joyful laughter.

Deciding where to hang the hammock can sometimes be complicated. Often rain forces me to rush to get that tart up. But today, the sky had finally cleared, and I did not have to hurry. I hunted for two trees the appropriate distance from each other, with no nearby leaning or dead trees that might fall on me. Of course, a good view is a bonus. In buggy weather, I want a breezy spot, and in chilly weather, I choose a sheltered area.

The warm sun encouraged me to swim. I swam far out, laid back and relaxed. Floating comes so easily that I could probably fall asleep out there on the lake.

Birds fascinate me, and I try to distinguish all the songs and sounds. Most birds are difficult to see, flitting high in the dense foliage.

Dark threatening clouds returned, persuading me to have an early dinner. Thunder rumbled. I crawled into my hammock with my gear safely stored beneath me. Blinding lightning flashed. Thunder roared and boomed louder and more constant for many hours. Somehow, I fell asleep.

*

A dreary day woke me. The morning fog progressed into a dismal, damp day. The threatening rain nixed my plan to paddle across this lake, take the portage to the west, and explore Hurdman Lake. Instead, I took the nearer portage to the east and hiked the one-kilometre portage to Loxley Lake. The little-used path wound up and down through the dense forest. The humidity made it feel like a sauna. As I peeled off my raincoat, the mosquitoes attacked. The path finally opened onto a secluded little lake. The view from this soft beach made the tormenting trek worth it.

Of course, once back on Laurel Lake, I also had a pretty view from my fire pit. I could relax on my little cushion with my back rammed against the big log bench and read my books. I watched four canoes travel the far side of the lake. Tall hemlocks, skinny red pines and magnificent white pines towered above me. Chipmunks hunting for food dared to come close. A red squirrel ran past me repeatedly, carrying big green pines cones in his mouth. A variety of birds serenaded. Even a hummingbird whizzed past. Peace and contentment transformed into joy. I felt so grateful to be out here in God's paradise with no barriers to separate me from all the life surrounding me.

In the night, another rumbling storm encompassed me yet again.

The morning sun shimmered on the lake's ripples, promising calm seas for my short trip back to Aura Lee Lake. I sure hoped both campsites would be free and the annoying motorboats would be gone.

The disappointment of hearing the roar while crossing the portage still could not take away my joy of being out here. My new home perched on the side of a hill near the narrow south end of the lake, making it impossible to see the noisy boats.

247

The sun soon dried the dampness from my gear caused by the two storms. I slid into the water for a swim.

This site needed some cleanup. At every campsite, I look for junk to stuff into my garbage bag. Thankfully there hasn't been much on this trip. This campfire held a pile of soggy bagels. Why? We are supposed to do whatever we can to prevent animals from being attracted to our campsite. Don't feed the wildlife. I keep my food safely enclosed in the bag, spray it with smelly bug repellant or sprinkle peppermint oil all over it since rodents do not like these odours, and maybe this can obscure the food aromas. Of course, I go through great pains to hang it for the night. You try finding the right branch and get that rope over it. You will realize my challenge.

As I relaxed in the warm sun with a book, a sleek blue and white Swift Keewaydin canoe glided by my site. As I pointed to my identical Serenity, I had to yell, "I love your canoe."

Another group with several lively teens and a couple of adults paddled past.

Everyone I meet in the park greets me with happy smiles and enthusiasm. Being surrounded by green life and freedom fills us all with a peaceful bond.

Night came too soon. Can you believe it? Again, another thunderstorm dumped rain on me most of the night. Seriously, what are the odds?

When heavy clouds block all starlight, I can't tell if my eyes are open or still closed. The nights can be extremely dark. But this time, when the calm returned, I looked out from under my tarp. A million lights danced all around me. What an extraordinary firefly performance. You never know when spectacular beauty will astound you.

*

Morning drizzle forced me to wear my ugly rain gear yet again. Oh, bother.

I packed up by 9:00 am. I did not hurry to leave this peaceful beauty. The wind at my back did not worry me.

No other travellers could be seen on my paddle back to the Brent campground.

As I approached the end of my trip, I remembered something essential. When you leave from a new area to which you will return, it is helpful to turn around and study what the shoreline looks like.

I paddled past what I thought would be the last peninsula but could see no parking lot, no Brent campground. Did I somehow pass it? I stayed close to shore, so that couldn't be possible. But surely, it had to be close. I felt like I had travelled so far down this huge Cedar Lake. Of course, the wind increased, and the drizzle continued.

I rounded another point and finally saw my destination. I slid onto the beach as a family prepared to start their adventure. With my gear stowed under a picnic table, I dug out my tiny umbrella and lunch and waited for Doug to pick me up.

The couple tried to contain the excitement of their young dog as they loaded lots of gear into their canoe. Their two little girls danced up and down the beach, looking for pretty stones. They all beamed with excitement. I felt so honoured when my new young friends shared their tiny treasures with me. I love stones too. The unique beauty in everything and everyone astounds me constantly.

Their trip began as mine ended. Doug arrived. He loaded my damp gear into and onto the car as I changed into clean, dry clothes. I always have a little bag stored in the car with clothes to wear when returning to civilization. We usually have dinner at a restaurant on the way home, and I am sure no one wants to see me in dirty, worn, stinky clothing.

As we ate, I entertained Doug with all my pictures and the whole story of my trek in the park. I had to ask him, "What are the odds that I should have a thunderstorm all three nights?"

I have so much rain during all my canoe trips that now my rain gear looks even uglier. Surely the odds of having good weather for my next trip will be good. Surely.

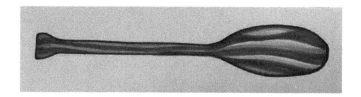

Can I Handle This New Challenge?

Kawayaymog Lake to Manitou Lake

Could I handle this new challenge of bigger lakes, longer portages, and a further distance than I had ever attempted before? Even though the rain tried to dampen my spirits, I felt very eager and a little nervous for my last canoe trip of this year.

Can you believe it? Rain again!

Of course, all my gear had been packed for days, except for the last-minute things and our breakfast to eat on the road.

By 5:00 am, Doug and I took off. We reached the far north-west corner of Algonquin Park, access point #1 at 8:00 am, Round Lake or Kawayaymog Lake. I think all the lakes should have their Algonquin names, don't you?

Cars and pick-ups filled the parking lot, but the park ranger assured me everyone would be leaving today, being Labour Day Monday.

At 9:00 am, Doug waved and took pictures as I left to cross the east end of this big lake. I could not stop smiling. I felt so free and excited. I easily found the entrance to the meandering Amble De Fond River. Paddling on lakes is straight-on. But rivers give such a fun variety with never-ending turns to practice different paddling tricks. Soon I had more paddling challenges as a long, constant parade of paddlers passed by. All headed out of the park.

Most rivers have many beaver dams. But I only encountered one in early construction, so I easily slid over it.

Rain turned to drizzle, which soon dissipated, and the sun tried to shine. Finally, I could pack away my ugly rain gear.

What a traffic jam on the two short portages. I hauled my big pack out of "Serenity," my canoe, and as I struggled to get it on my back, a middle-aged man and two teenage girls offered to take my canoe across the portage. Wow. What fun to have help. I thanked them greatly. I really wished I could ask if they could meet me on the longest portage of my trip. Joking.

At the end of the second portage stood a tall stone memorial. Scattered throughout the park, you can find many reminders of the history of this vast wilderness: old logging camp tools, barely visible building foundations, and remains of train trestles and rail beds.

As I waited for an opening in the crowd of paddlers at the take-out into North Tea Lake-West Arm, or Kawayaskigamog Lake, I checked my map and wondered which campsite I should head for. I hoped for one near the far end. With so many campers heading out of the park, it appeared that I could have my pick of many vacant sites.

Out on this big lake, I headed down the centre, finally passing by a big island. I had many vacant sites to explore and choose from. At 12:30 pm, I chose the single site on the small island. This had an easy sandy take-out, tall white pine trees, the perfect spot for my hammock and an excellent view from the fire pit. I felt full of childlike glee, and the big smile never left my face.

Lunchtime. I had the rest of the day to enjoy a swim, relax, read, and snack on my favourite treat, dark chocolate-covered almonds. Oh yea!

My relaxation ended abruptly when a red squirrel high above me in the white pine tree bombed me with sticky green pinecones. "Hey, stop that!"

After the multitude of campers that I encountered leaving the lake, I saw no one else, no other humans. Besides this noisy, pretty, little red squirrel and a curious chipmunk, I also had the company of a large black and white piliated woodpecker, raucous ravens, noisy blue jays, talkative chick-a-dees, beautiful loons and a family of common merganser ducks.

A great variety of ducks hide somewhere in our wilderness but are rarely seen. The common mergansers must be bolder as they often swim by.

Stars flooded the dark night sky. This spectacular scene always overwhelms me with wonder at the vastness of our universe and the power of a Creator that just spoke it all into being.

*

The bright morning sun promised a warm and calm day. I must be getting better at packing up because I headed out at 8:30 am, much earlier than usual. I hoped to find my new campsite on the far end of North Tea Lake-East Arm. I passed many scenic campsites with soft beaches, and others perched high on rocky island lookouts. By 11:00 am, I found a rocky peninsula site just as the wind began to pick up. Sturdy cedars made a good shelter for my tarp and hammock. I enjoyed my lunch and my view of this large lake as I watched a few paddlers pass by. The wind made me feel too chilled for a swim, so I reinforced the fire pit, gathered firewood, and watched a tiny mole wandering through the dead leaves in the forest.

The winds increased. The clouds filled the sky, growing darker and more ominous. I watched a couple paddle by, fighting the waves to the campsite just beyond mine in a sheltered bay.

I secured all my gear safely under my hammock and used the canoe to hold down my extra little tarp, hoping to protect my small shelter from the coming rain. The wind gained power. I lay in my hammock and watched the trees dance as darkness descended. No silence during this night as the wind crashed waves onto my rocky shore and the trees clashed. Rain pelted down. The wind grew violent. My poor tarp had already suffered damage on an earlier trip. This time I wondered if this insane wind would rip it away altogether. I lay there trying to devise some plan to keep dry if my tarp took off.

But I felt no fear. I always have options. I had to get out of the warm bed, reinforce my ropes, and better secure the canoe and all my gear. What a wild, wet night.

*

By morning the sky had cleared, the sun shone, and the wind had calmed but not stopped.

I felt excited and so happy to be exploring new wilderness. I had a quick paddle to reach the short portage into Manitou Lake. The wind had grown and tried to slam me into the big boulders that blocked the path's entrance. I managed to get the canoe and gear to land without injury. Maybe a gymnast with good balance could better avoid an ankle injury. But, hey, I wanted a new challenge, right?

Well, another challenge loomed before me. The first half of this four hundred-metre portage went steeply uphill. Oh my.

257

Tired and winded, I made it down the other side. Here the waves seemed not as wild. I checked my map to plan my crossing, hoping to get near the far end of this enormous lake. I had just begun paddling when the wind gained power, the waves grew violent, and the clouds darkened.

Thunder. Yikes. Plan B. Race for the nearest vacant campsite. I didn't have far to go to find one on a high point bordered by big rocks, which prevented a speedy exit. I struggled to keep my balance while preventing Serenity from smashing against the rocks as I hoisted my gear and chucked it up onto the shore. What a dance I had to perform to get Serenity into a safe position to survive the coming storm.

The thunder rumbled. The clouds darkened. I rushed to get protected under my tarp. I won that contest. Sitting dry in my little shelter, I could watch the lightning show all around while I enjoyed my lunch and coffee.

The rain poured, quickly creating streams rushing down the hill and off my tarp. I had to dig trenches to keep the flood away from my feet and gear. Finally, the storm passed by, but the wind increased. I guess I would not be travelling on to the end of this huge lake today, with such crazy wind and waves.

Finally, the sun returned, and I could explore my site and check out my excellent view from this high point. To the west, I could almost see the entrance to the steep portage. Directly south, I could hear the waterfalls at another, longer portage to the north Tea Lake East Arm. To the west, islands and another peninsula prevented me from seeing the entire length of this large lake.

I eventually found the thunderbox, which had walls. To help others find this obscure trail, I trimmed the path a little and made a big rock arrow on the ground, pointing the way. I discovered massive boulders here and there, a deep mossy valley and many tall fallen trees. Most sites have paths along the shoreline. Discovering the huge piles of moose scat makes me wonder how often these massive creatures come here.

The wind grew, zipping away the sun's warmth. Whitecaps smashed onto my rocky shore. I found a sunny spot to prop my chair and relaxed against a tall red pine to read. I usually bring a couple of tiny books, Star Trek and "The Good Book," the Bible. I also have a card deck with survival information on each card.

259

After finding a suitable branch to hang my food bag, I secured everything for the night. Clouds moved in. The chilly wind continued, and drizzle blew in all night.

*

The crazy wind thrashed my tarp and woke me to a morning of dark clouds. I had to keep my rain gear on to keep out the chill. Making a fire with damp wood is quite a challenge. I could cook with my little propane stove, but today I attempted to warm up with a fire.

Waves smashed onto my rocky shore, which made getting in and out of the water a treacherous task. I chose not to swim. But out here in the wilderness, I am always a happy camper.

I had hoped to get to the far end of this large lake yesterday. Today the strong wind and waves prevented me from getting anywhere safely or easily. The plan had been to camp at the far northeast end of Manitou Lake tonight so that tomorrow I could head down a long portage to stay on Amble De Fond River for my last night. On my last day, I would get picked up on Kioshkokwi Lake at the Kiosk campground.

The park rule states that you should always camp on the lake you have booked. But the thunderstorm and this incessant wind prevented me from following through with my best-laid plans. Since I saw few paddlers, I thought I could rearrange my plans without taking anyone's reserved spot. Plan B. Head back to North Tea Lake tomorrow and camp on the West Arm for my last night in the park.

Doug provided me with a satellite phone, so I could keep him updated and reassure him that I am alive. Now I had to let him know my change of plans and to pick me up on Kawaywamog Lake in two days.

With lots of wood gathered for my use and extra for the next campers to visit here, I could enjoy my small fire and roast marshmallows. Packing up what I could that evening, I hoped for no wind for the next day of paddling the big lakes.

*

Dense morning fog erased any view. The wind had vanished as well. By the time I had packed and loaded Serenity, the fog had lifted, and I headed off to hike the hill to North Tea Lake. I so enjoy paddling. The rhythmic strokes set me in tune with the pulse of this wonderful paradise. Life is realigned. Energy and joy are restored.

As I rounded the peninsula that marks the entrance into the West Arm of North Tea Lake, I met an influx of campers. Oh my. I had not realized that this weekend could bring so many into the park's interior. I felt

262

confident that I would still find an open site since I wanted to be closer to the west end, and surely all others would travel further east.

Just as the wind increased and my energy drained, I found a good site with a small beach, a big fire pit, a counter created out of sticks and many choice spots for my hammock.

The sunshine ensured me that this time I did not have to make a mad dash to hang my tarp. This time I could enjoy my leisurely lunch and coffee. I explored this large peninsula and relaxed in the sun on the warm beach.

Of course, I had to text Doug on the satellite phone to let him know I made it here. He warned me that the forecast for tomorrow included high winds, beginning in the early afternoon, followed by a thunderstorm. Yikes. Not again.

Yet, I still enjoyed every minute of this day.

For my last morning on a canoe trip, I plan for a slow, relaxed morning. But this time, I would have to leave as early as possible. I prepared as well as I could that evening. I do not need a reason to crawl early into my cozy bed. I peacefully enjoyed the view of the lake, listened to the loons and hoped to hear an owl in the silent night.

*

A stunning sunrise greeted me. I did not want to leave. But sometimes the forecast is correct, so I wolfed down a power bar as I rushed to pack. I had Serenity loaded by 8:00 am. My hope for light winds vanished as I slid out of my secluded little bay. The wind promised a hard workout en route to the first portage. Paddling into the wind makes progress slow. I had a race to win.

As I completed the second portage, I discovered that the water level had dropped. How could this happen? Speed is impossible when paddling in shallow water. After a few bends in the river, I discovered the cause. The beaver dam I had so easily slid over on my first day had grown two feet high. I had to climb out and haul the loaded canoe over. Those beavers certainly had been busy in these six days.

A few more twists in the river and the terrain opened to the extensive bog. I could feel the wind increase. When I made the final turn onto the open lake, the powerful wind pushed me backwards. I fought to get onto the open water. But I already felt weary. I had to pull up onto a nearby beach to rest. I slumped onto the soothing sand. How could I continue? The wild wind and huge white-capped waves crashed against me. I would have to fight my way diagonally across the dangerous waves to get back to the parking lot. I knew the direction but could not see it from this distance. A long struggle against the powerful forces of nature faced me.

I had no choice. The winds would only grow worse as the storm approached. I had to get back into Serenity and continue the race. I enjoy a challenge, right?

I pushed hard. Stroke, stroke, stroke. If I paused for just a moment to catch my breath, I would be forced backward or sideways to the raging waves, which could quickly capsize me. I felt like a sock sloshed about in a frantic washing machine. Serenity kept stable despite the turbulent lake. How long had I been struggling?

I felt no fear in my narrow, tippy canoe. Oh, wait. One fear triggered a whisper of nauseous panic. What if I became too exhausted to eat lunch?

As I inched agonizingly towards the far shore, I could finally see my destination and Doug pacing on the beach. Finally, the swells calmed slightly when I entered a more sheltered lee of the lake. As I rammed Serenity into the sand, Doug grabbed the bow and pulled me out of the waves.

I just wanted to collapse onto the warm beach, but I had to hug Doug first. I discovered that I had been working strenuously for more than five hours. So tired, but not too tired to eat. Never. In fact, I felt exhilarated. I did it. I survived massive waves, a steep portage, a thunderstorm, and insane winds.

I experienced wonder in the stunning sunrise and sunsets, powerful peace in the silence and joyful surprise in all the surrounding beauty. I felt the presence of the mighty Creator with me.

Where will I go next year?

Eight-Day Solo Trip

Smoke Lake to Lake of Two Rivers

Was I ready for this, my longest in time and distance solo canoe trip? I would love to say, "I was born ready," but then you would all ask, "Why did it take you so long to do this?" In one month, I would be seventy.

Any adventure has questions, uncertainties, and challenges. Was I really ready for this? Was I fit enough to handle these longer and more difficult portages? Did I have the endurance to paddle longer distances? Would it be too buggy, too muddy? Would it be too crowded with campers to find good campsites?

Oh, I know some of you will look at my route and realize that most people can do this distance in two days. But I will need to take my time, and I want to enjoy all the beauty and each campsite.

At 7:00 am, June 10, I loaded my canoe for an eight-day solo canoeing adventure. The grey sky and drizzle could not dampen my enthusiasm. But at least I had nice new rain gear, finally. This early in the morning, the big Smoke Lake had little wind. Since this is probably a busier starting point for canoe trips in Algonquin Park, I wondered how many people I would meet. Would I find nice open breezy sites to keep the bugs away? After crossing the easy portage into Ragged Lake, I met six loaded canoes headed out of Algonquin Park. Travelling past many vacant campsites, I found the one I had hoped for, perched high above a pebbly beach. This site had tall red and white pines, a beautiful view and sat close to the portage I would cross the next day.

268

The clouds dispersed as I set up camp, and the sun warmed and dried me and my gear. Two years earlier, when my friend Linda and I camped here, I had hung my hammock very near the fire pit from two massive white pine trees. A huge bare branch on the ground caused me to look up and see that the top half of one of these trees was dead. Thankfully I had many healthy trees to choose from.

Another problem became evident. A swamp totally prevented any access to the thunderbox. Oh bother!

I had time to enjoy the warm afternoon. And so did someone else. Right beside my canoe, a giant snapping turtle chose to lay her eggs in the sand. I did not want to disturb her on her important mission. Most Ontario turtles are endangered. Their young face many dangers. Foxes, raccoons, and mink will dig up and eat the eggs. Many other predators endanger them before these hatchlings make it into the water. Turtles do not reproduce until they are almost twenty years old. If they survive, they can live well over one hundred years. They all have such artistic colours and patterns. We have so much to learn about our wilderness neighbours. Turtles seem to take their time and enjoy life. Maybe we should learn from them, as well.

In the darkness, I listened to three different kinds of owls: the hawk owl, the barred owl, and the long-eared owl. Amazing!

*

Early the next sunny morning, a catbird serenaded me with his entire repertoire of songs while I packed up. They repeat the songs of all the other birds they have heard. Amazing!

I soon reached the dreaded "devil's staircase" portage. Beautiful tiny violets adorned the first step. I think the devil has no flowers, so I will just call this "the staircase." I had prepared long and hard for this long steep climb. Enough, I hoped. I took my time and rested often. No worries.

Elated to have it completed, I took off to paddle Big Porcupine Lake. Halfway along, I slid my butt off the seat and onto the canoe floor, rested my legs on the big pack lying in the bow of the canoe and let a gentle breeze sail me down the length of a long and narrow section. I enjoyed the vibrant spring green trees and greeted some painted turtles sunning on logs. Soon enough, I had to sit up and hunt for the small, easy portage to Bonnechere Lake. Curiosity about Bonnechere Lake had been the incentive for planning this route. I must visit Bonnechere Lake because I live on the Bonnechere River, which strangely has no connection to this lake.

This pretty lake had some rocky cliff shorelines. The first campsite did not have enough open area to blow the bugs away. The second site had campers, so I happily took the third, which proved even better than the one I had the previous night. How thankful am I? The rocky point had easy water access, beautiful cedars to hang my hammock and even a log bench with a back on it. The aroma of pines and cedars and the breeze blowing across the lake rejuvenated me after the long workout.

This warm sunny afternoon tempted me for a swim, although I rarely need tempting as I love to swim. But the icy temperature of the water caused me to jump out immediately.

I waved at two canoes passing by with four young ladies. Later another canoe arrived on the lake and took the first campsite.

I piled some firewood, hunted for the right branch for the food bag, then relaxed on the bench and enjoyed the sun's warmth.

This big day of paddling and portaging meant, of course, that bedtime came early. I felt thankful to have a few layers to wear that chilly night, and then I easily fell asleep listening to the multitude of tiny spring peeper frogs.

*

Rain returned in the night. It stopped long enough for me to get packed up in the early morning. The drizzle resumed staying with me all the while I paddled and portaged. But the beauty surrounding me always makes me feel sunny. I paddled the length of Bonnechere Lake and portaged to Phipps Lake. Another short paddle brought me to an easy walk to Kirkwood Lake.

After crossing this small lake, I had a long, horrendous, and torturous trip on the portage to Pardee Lake. This wore me out more than any other part of this trip. Over seven hundred metres of up and down, slippery rocks and roots, and mostly deep, dark, stinky, sucky muck. Sucky muck causes you to sink and attempts to swallow your shoes. There was no way to get around all the deep mud. While I carried my heavy pack, I slipped a few times. No matter how carefully I walked, I was doomed. I fell into the ankle-deep mud. Laying on my back with my pack deep into the muck, I felt like an inverted turtle, unable to move. Wiggling to loosen the straps, I detached myself, crawled in the mud and struggled to stand. I yanked my pack out of the stinky dark mud, put it back on and attempted to get to the end of this torture. Someone should have videoed me in that hilarious slapstick comedy!

Of course, I had to go back and get the canoe. Oh, I would be extra careful with my footing this time. No. It didn't help. I slowly slid sideways all the way back into the muck. Muddier, more tired. I had to stand deep in the muck and try to get my canoe back on my head. Realizing that the rest of the portage path consisted of deep wet sludge, I just dragged Serenity the rest of the way.

Finally, I thankfully made it to little Pardee Lake, which only had two campsites. The one perched on a huge, long, smooth rock peninsula made a choice easy. What a beautiful campsite, easy take out, fantastic view, and perfect tree to hang my hammock. Exhausted, I made camp in very slow motion, and I felt so grateful that I would stay here for two nights.

The dark clouds dissipated, and the warm sun came out to help dry me. I crawled into my hammock extra early. Sleep did not come so quickly. "No-see-ums," almost invisible, tiny biting flies, tortured me for a long time. I don't know how so many could get into my little net-protected bed. No amount of bug repellent would detour them. They even bit through the bug net covering my head. I finally fell asleep in spite of the painful stinging bites.

*

The morning mist hung over the mirror-calm lake that bright, warm, cloudless day. So healing. So cheering. I cleaned up my muddy gear and spread it all over the huge, smooth rock peninsula to dry. I guess my waterproof pack is not mud-proof.

I took my time to enjoy all the beauty surrounding me. Stunning spring flowers, new vibrant green growth of moss, trees, and ferns. There is such variety in everything. I bring tiny, laminated brochures and cards from the Algonquin Park Visitor's Center to help me learn the names of the various ferns, flowers, and birds. I have seen and heard loons on every Algonquin Lake.

June is a pretty month, usually with hot weather and many spring flowers. This part of Ontario is notorious for spring bugs: mosquitoes, black flies, deer flies, and horse flies. Most of the time, I only had to deal with the mosquitoes on the portages. I rarely had any bugs at my open breezy campsites. The worst of all these bugs are the "no-see-ums." They sure can sting for something barely visible. Somehow, they managed to get through my hammock's bug net and tortured me through the night.

Tiny bumps covered my face, and I had a black eyelid. Luckily, no one saw me for many days. Still, I would rather deal with spring bugs than people on the busy portages of mid-summer. Oh, dear.

Bedtime came early again. My hammock feels so cozy to relax while watching the light fade away. A clear sky let the full moon brighten the night. The nights are so spectacular.

"The heavens declare the glory of God."

*

Morning came bright and calm, with my energy restored. I packed up as a Canada goose family came to visit with their three tiny, fuzz-ball new babies. They busied themselves eating in the grasses along the shore only a few feet from me. I tried to move very slowly and quietly to avoid disturbing them here in their home.

My tiny cook stove sat close by, heating water for breakfast. The geese approached too close, and I had to do something to keep them away. But I still did not want to scare them. Sitting on the red pine needle carpet, I slowly slid to the stove. Daddy goose kept his eye on me since he stood only five feet on the opposite side of the stove. He hissed a warning, but only once, then slowly moved his family away just as the water came to a boil and I could make my tea and porridge.

I do enjoy my tea and porridge, which has not only oats but chia and flax seeds, quinoa flakes and dried blueberries.

I so enjoyed my visit with the geese. I didn't mind the late start this day since I only had a short paddle and one short, easy portage. Then came the hunt for my new campsite. No worries. I had no competition. I saw no paddlers this day, either. I did see loons on every lake. So beautiful.

Good thing I checked my map, or I may have headed out the wrong way. Although on this small lake, it would be a slight detour, and I would soon realize my mistake. Sometimes it is possible to get mixed up, leading to a much longer day and frustration instead of bliss. Check your map. Bring a compass.

The little portage went around a beautiful waterfall. So much beauty everywhere. Did I say that already? Come and see.

I took my time paddling Harness Lake looking for the few campsites. A few were marked for the Highland trail backpackers. At the top end of the lake, I found a fantastic site on the east side of the island. A few common merganser ducks rested on the smooth rocky point. With an easy take-out and a large, level, open area, I quickly found a perfect spot for my hammock and the best tree branch ever to hang the food bag. I don't know why people call it a bear hang or a bear bag because it is for my food, not the bear.

Even with my late start, I had lots of time to enjoy the new home this day. Of course, I first set up my tarp and hammock. I enjoyed a leisurely lunch and collected some firewood. I never burn much more than a few twigs and sticks, but the rule is, "Leave the campsite better than you find it." I always collect more wood than I use and pick up any garbage. But on this trip, I saw no trash. Wonderful. I did find some rope at a couple of sites this trip which came in handy. Fun find.

The water still felt too icy cold to let me swim long. I jumped in and out. Refreshing! I had time to relax, read, and listen to all the spring songbirds.

Later I prepared for the forecasted rain. More rain. The no-see-ums tormented me again, but I finally fell asleep to the harmonious bullfrogs. A phenomenal full moon brightened the night.

*

I woke in time to catch a wonderfully colourful sunrise. While I packed up, the dark grey clouds stole any colour, and I put on my rain gear again. No worries. All my gear is packed in dry sacks and stuffed into my big backpack.

Today I would only have a five-minute paddle to reach the longest portage I have ever done. Could I handle it? Had I trained well enough to survive this? The map assured me that it had no significant inclines and mainly went downhill. I would take my time, and my pack must surely be lighter now with a lot of my food eaten.

The portage travelled over many planks and logs, crossing wet areas and mostly level paths through the forest, long but not hard. The clouds grew darker, and the drizzle turned to rain. As I emerged from under the dense trees to the open river, a male common merganser skidded onto the water directly in front of me. Wow. These guys are very similar to loons with their black backs and white bellies, but their long narrow beaks are bright red. He travelled downriver as I attempted to load my canoe. What a challenge to get a heavy backpack into a narrow canoe while balancing on wobbly rocks. Rocks everywhere. Poor Serenity, more scratches and scrapes.

Just as I struggled to climb aboard, deep booming thunder threatened. I had to pull my canoe back onto shore and drag my gear back into a semi-protected, partially dry spot under a tree. Then I dug out my tiny umbrella. There I sat unbothered by the company of many mosquitoes with my head bug net on. Do I just sit here then? How long? When I had heard no rumbling for a while, I hoped it would now be safe to paddle. The dreaded thunder growled again as soon as I began to haul my gear down to the river. Back under the tree. Bored now. I dug out my water and snacks and waited.

No lightning had threatened, and the thunder grew faint and finally ended. I loaded up Serenity again and took off, not even bothering to take off the bug net. I easily slid over two beaver dams on this very narrow, winding creek. By the time I reached the open water of Head Lake, the hard rain quickly put inches of water at my feet and made visibility difficult, with the drops plastering the net onto my streaked glasses. I could barely make out the campsite signs. I didn't have far to find one that looked good from the little I could actually see. A huge round bolder marked the entrance. My wet feet and hands chilled me. Since my tarp always gets packed at the top of my big pack, I quickly put it up. Then I made a ring of rocks, gathered semi-dry twigs, and yanked out a fire starter, lighter and my chair. I sat protected under my tarp, with a tiny fire to warm my hands and feet and surveyed what I could see of my new home.

Even though I felt exhausted and soggy, I also felt gratified to have survived my longest portage and to have discovered this excellent campsite. And I didn't die due to lightning.

Soon the sky brightened, the clouds dissipated, and the warm sun returned. Free to explore my site, I felt confident that this must be the best campsite on this lake. On a long point, the tall pines made a colourful orange-red carpet, and cedars made sturdy trees to hang my tarp and hammock. A tall rock ledge protected the large firepit from the growing wind. What an excellent site. I didn't even have far to walk far to the thunderbox.

I hung my wet shoes, socks, and rain gear to dry in the wind and sun, then I collected firewood and made supper, feeling so thankful for this beautiful home for the next two nights.

I waved to four canoes passing by, near the far shore. I wondered if they would stay on this lake or find the portage to the next one.

That evening I discovered a hole in my hammock's bug net, stuffed it with a bit of tissue and then slept so well, free of the tiny tormenting, stinging bugs. I heard another thunderstorm approach. Lightening flashed in the dark night. But it only stayed long enough for a brief light shower. Later the sky cleared for the big moon to brighten my wilderness home.

*

What a wonderful warm sunny morning, my last full day of this, my longest solo canoe trip.

I surely had packed too much food and would have loved to spend an extra two days here. But my toilet paper would only last one more day. Drat!

The bright sun warmed me, so I took off my hoodie. The chilly wind intensified, so I put it back on. Then I found a protected spot to sit and removed the hoodie again, but because of the narrow neck, each time I pulled it over my head, it messed up my hair and attempted to rip my nose off. The crazy wind grew until white caps covered the lake. I watched two paddlers arriving from Head Creek struggle to cross the lake. But the strength of the wind and waves forced them back to the nearest campsite.

I truly enjoyed every moment of this day of rest. I relaxed on my tiny inflatable cushion on the ground. I leaned against the life jacket beside a gigantic pine tree to read, write in my journal, and study the lake with my binoculars. Wonderful beauty. Just sit and be renewed and filled with peace. Be still and grow closer to the Creator.

I had time to explore. A steep path travelled up a tall hill just behind the campsite. You would think that I had done enough physical work in the past six days, enough hiking on all the portages since I double-carried them all. But I felt energized and curious, so up and up and up I went. Near the top, I found stunning treasures. Spectacular colourful shelf fungus grew on a tall old dead stump. What a beautiful paradise. What wonderful peace. What an awesome Creator! His phenomenal artistry in all His creation demonstrates His passionate love for it all.

I surely loved these days of challenging workouts, breathtaking scenery, surprising beauty and healing peace. I didn't really want it to end. But I couldn't wait to share my adventures with Doug and show everyone my pictures. Overwhelmed with this incredible experience, gratitude flooded my soul.

Supper cooked as I organized my gear in preparation for tomorrow's departure. My plan for my last day had been to have a leisurely morning and take time to enjoy breakfast. I like to have plans and stick to them. But having had five very unique children and a husband who likes spontaneity, I have learned to be flexible. The forecast warned me of growing winds for tomorrow with the possibility of an afternoon thunderstorm. The threat of lighting makes any water travel deadly. The wind would not be a problem paddling the two rivers, but I did have to begin tomorrow by crossing half of this Head Lake. Watching the two guys struggle today, I didn't want that much of a challenge. Been there, done that on another solo trip.

I tried to stay up late enough to get one sunset picture, but my hammock is just too comfy, and I do so enjoy laying there watching the light disappear, and the silent darkness descend.

*

A robin woke me with the first morning light. Or did the noisy tarp flapping in the wind wake me? Oh no, not wind already. I reluctantly crawled out of my warm comfort to face a busy day, the last day of my longest solo canoe trip. I gobbled down a few bites of breakfast while

289

packing up. Thankfully the sun shone with the promise of warm temperatures.

Before 7:00 am, I gave the huge boulder on the shore a farewell hug and headed Serenity into the wind and growing waves. Oh yes, I struggled, and I worked hard to make any headway at all. What should have been a ten-minute leisurely paddle turned into a long, difficult challenge.

I knew today would take time, meandering the two rivers, so I sure didn't appreciate starting exhausted. I turned onto the narrow bay, and thankfully the wind pushed me towards the portage into Head Creek. Creeks and rivers provide a totally different adventure than lake travel. Constant winding, you never know what will be around the next curve. Will you scare ducks into flight? See a blue heron catching a snack? Meet curious otters? Run into a beaver dam to haul yourself over? Will the river open into a boggy area or narrow to swiftly flow between rocky shores? Or maybe glide past a swampy area and find a massive moose?

Yes, soon enough, in my morning travels, I spied a cow moose before she noticed me. I stopped paddling and silently grabbed my camera as I slowly drifted closer. But before I could get near enough for a good picture, she saw me and disappeared into the dense forest. Wow! So amazing. Such a blessing to see these huge creatures. This peaceful, beautiful encounter rejuvenated me. What more wonders might I meet?

All the five short portages I had that day took me around spectacular waterfalls. So loud. So powerful. I told you, beauty is everywhere! Come and see! Take your time to discover and enjoy.

"God saw all that He had made and said, "It is good." Genesis 1:25.

"We give thanks to You, O God, we give thanks! For Your wondrous works declare that Your name is near." Psalms 75:1.

I see unique beauty everywhere I look in all of God's amazing, artistic creation, in each creature and every person.

On my third portage, I sat in the shade, had an energy bar, and guzzled some water. Even though these portages were short and easy, hauling the heavy pack in and out of my narrow canoe felt like a struggle. The forceful current at the narrow take-outs and put-ins tried to wrench Serenity from my grasp. But, hey, I love a challenge, right?

I dawdled on my last and shortest portage. My amazing eight-day solo trip would soon be over. What a wonderful trip. When can I go again? Where could I go next?

The current rushed me onward and shoved me onto Lake of Two Rivers. I left my campsite before 7:00 am and reached my last short stretch just before 1:00 pm. The wind tried to hurl me across to the far side of the lake, but I held my course and soon heard Doug yell a greeting. As I slid onto the beach, I didn't know if I could jump out and hug Doug or collapse on the beach, exhausted. But the realization that I had completed such an extraordinary journey replaced my fatigue with a feeling of fantastic triumph.

I canoe it!

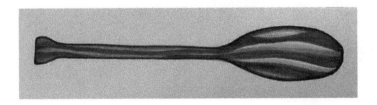

Helpful Hints:
(Bossy Me)

1. Learn some tips from the experts. That would not be me.
Kevin Callan "The Happy Camper", has a wealth of insight,
information, and humour. I so enjoy his video called "Learn to laugh at
yourself." While watching, Doug says, "This makes me feel exhausted." I
am compelled to say, "I want to do this!" To which my friends exclaim,
"Why?"

I hope you catch the passion.

It seems not everyone who attempts canoe camping necessarily knows
how to paddle a canoe. What? Please get some paddling tips, YouTube
lessons, or at least watch some experienced paddlers before taking a trip.
You will be surprised by the ease and variety of paddling strokes.

Watching novice paddlers exhausts me. Come on people. Two people
in a canoe need to work as a team with synchronized strokes on opposite
sides. Flipping randomly from one side to the other causes zig-zagging all
the way down the lake and multiplies the distance. Of course, one person
may be stronger than the other, so a little cooperation is needed. Usually,
the bigger person sits in the stern and is the more powerful paddler, so he
can easily compensate by doing a J stroke to keep you headed straight. Get
a good rhythm that you both feel comfortable with. Yay team!

2. Plan ahead, far, far ahead.

When it comes to wilderness camping, you must let the Park know which lakes you wish to camp on each specific date. I phoned the Algonquin Park reservations office two weeks prior to my first hoped-for canoe trip. You can stop laughing. Now I know you must make your interior camping reservations five months in advance.

- Plan your route. Know exactly where you want to go. Reserve far in advance.
- Length. How many days do you have?
- Know your limitations and strengths. Please do not make it too challenging. Make it enjoyable.
- Goals. To go where few have gone before, or just where you have not gone before?

3. **Bring a good waterproof map**, compass and small binoculars.

Keep your map, compass, and binoculars within reach of the navigator. Searching the shoreline for a portage or campsite sign is not as easy as I thought. A portage sign could be hidden behind a tree branch, depending on your vantage point. It can seem even impossible to distinguish any opening or trail due to the dense forest. Green, green everywhere and not a path to see. Is it a bay or the opening to the river you are looking for? Or is it an island or a peninsula ahead of you?

There are a few options of water-tight clear plastic bags for the map and your camera, which can hang around your neck or be attached to a pack in front of the navigator.

There are a number of tech options as well. Download the map app onto your phone or a satellite phone with a GPS.

4. **Safety:**

- Bring a well-supplied first aid kit: bandages of various sizes, disinfectant, aloe vera (for burns and sunburns), tensor bandages of multiple sizes, Benadryl, aspirin (or pain reliever of your choice), small scissors and tweezers, sunscreen, bug repellant.

- The most common injuries while wilderness camping are **ankle injuries and burns.**

- Fire makes pots extremely HOT! Bring stove mitts (work gloves) for cooking.

- Wear a hat and a thin long-sleeved top to avoid sunburn and sunstroke.

- Watch every step you take; rocks and roots are everywhere. If you want to look around, first stop, then look.

- NEVER RUN.

5. **Be bear aware.** Take all the precautions.

I make everyone camping with me **wear a whistle at all times**. No critter, man or beast likes loud noises. Whistles can be incredibly loud and will scare the bear away. Whistles can be good for summoning help or warning other campers. Do most people know the Morse code for help? S.O.S.: three short, three long and three short blasts.

Kevin Callan tells a story of how he detoured a bear's approach by whacking his paddle on a big flat rock. Use your extra paddle or a big stick. Don't break your only paddle.

Some recommend bear spray, but I have heard that wasp spray is more effective. However, you must make sure the wind is not blowing toward you. If the spray blows into your face, then you will be defenceless instead of detouring the bear. A whistle is easier to carry at all times.

Take all the safety measures. Hang up your food pack safely. Include in that your toiletries and soaps. To a bear, these may smell yummy too.

A food barrel keeps your food safe from rain and maybe smaller critters. A bear can still damage a barrel, so it must be hoisted high and safe. I use a dry sack. I spray cedar oil, peppermint oil, or bug repellent on the outside, as this will hopefully mask the smell of the foods that may attract any critter.

Clean all your pots safely. Do not put ANY soap in the lake or river. Soap is hazardous to all things living in the water. Even if it says biodegradable. Bring a pot or pail of water into the forest, wash your dishes there and dump the soapy, crumbly, greasy water into the thunderbox.

6. What to do about water?

Way back in the day, you could just dip your cup into the lake and drink, no worries. Not so now. I don't understand that even when you think you are far from industry and pollution, the water may still not be safe. You are still not that far from industry. Much logging is still being done in the park.

So how do you have safe drinking water?

There are many options. Filter and boil. Takes too long.

Bleach tablets. This just doesn't sound healthy to me.

There are various water filters, purifiers, pumps, and ultraviolet light sterilizers. Ask the experts like Kevin Callan, who has videos on the easy and compact options.

7. What about food?

I suggest vegan foods as they are less likely to attract bears. Maybe. Bears do like peanut butter. And so do chipmunks, I found out.

Outfitters sell dehydrated meal packets. Your local grocery store now sells various dried meal packets: Indian curry chickpeas, Mexican chilli beans and rice, Chinese mushroom rice, pasta and packets of Alfredo or cheddar sauce. (Vegan version for me.) You can also dehydrate your own meals of soups, sauces, and stews. Pitas, wraps, and naan are flat and don't take up much space. I measure ingredients for pancakes, Bannock, and porridge into labelled baggies. Powdered milk, instant coffee, teas, and sugar also get put into baggies. Then each day's meals are placed together, putting the last day's meal on the bottom of the bag or barrel. I usually have extra snacks like nuts, dried fruit, granola, and protein bars. Of course, the coffee goes on top.

Remember, no glass or tins. I have an assortment of small plastic containers with tight-fitting lids for things like peanut butter, cooking oil and maple syrup.

Hang up the food bag. Finding a suitable tree can be difficult. It must not be near your tent. It must have a long enough branch so that you can hang it three feet from the trunk and any other tree and high enough to be nine feet off the ground. The branch must be strong enough to hold all your food.

I have discovered that getting the rope around the branch is not so easy for me. Use a small cloth bag or an old sock, place a rock into it and tie it to the end of your rope. Throw it over the branch, remembering that what goes up will come down. Ouch! I have narrowly avoided injury and learned quite a bit through mishaps. When you finally get the rope in place, remove the rock bag and attach the long rope to the food bag/barrel and hoist away. Tie the other end securely around the base of a tree.

At a couple of sites, we found a cable had been strung high between two good trees equipped with a hook and winch. How easy is that?

Please talk to the experts before going wilderness canoe camping. Check out Kevin Callan's videos on all things camping: hanging the food bag, packing food, camping gear, paddling strokes, bugs and bears.

8. What to pack?

But what do I really know, anyway?

• A good backpack.

If your backpack is not waterproof, everything must be packed in plastic bags and sealed well. It is better for your back if you place the lighter things at the bottom and the heavier stuff at the top. The pack should ride high on your back, not bounce on your butt. Straps holding it secure helps your posture. Your back will thank you.

- Map and compass.
- First aid kit.
- One tee shirt, one pair of shorts, one sweatshirt, and one pair of long pants (sweatpants?) One long thin light, coloured top and one long thin pants (in case of sunburn or cold temps requiring layers). Two pairs of socks and undies.
- Rain gear, swimsuit, small towel, sun hat, running shoes, and maybe water shoes? Sandals may not be the safest.
- An unbreakable water bottle.
- Food, cooking gear: stove, dishes, cutlery, water purifier, matches, a tarp and a tiny tent or hammock.
- A whistle, flashlight, binoculars, camera, and enough toilet paper.
- Sleeping bag and a tiny pillow or roll up your sweatshirt or towel for a pillow. A shrink bag is such a good help for packing the sleeping bag and clothes.
- Optional luxuries: a small book, deck of cards, tiny umbrella, and tiny camp chair.

Pack the following to be easily accessible:

- Water bottle.
- First aid kit.

Include sunscreen, bug repellant, disinfectant, different-sized bandages; tensor wraps for ankles or elbows, and tweezers. Be tick aware. The Park and Google have good information on how to deal with ticks.

- Rain gear.
- One toilet paper roll.

If there is no thunderbox nearby, and a moment of some urgency hits you, run into the bush, dig a hole, and then cover it and bring an extra plastic bag for your soiled toilet paper. Leave no trace, no litter.

- When paddling, keep a good waterproof map and compass in front of the navigator.
- Everyone wears a whistle at all times.

I usually wear my swimsuit under a light long-sleeved shirt and long thin pants. Wear a hat. Protect yourself from sunburn, sunstroke out on the water and bugs in the bush.

Good shoes are essential for portages. Pine needles and mud can be slippery, and rocks and roots can make your trek treacherous. Remember, we want to avoid ankle injuries. Thin or open shoes could also make broken toes a threat.

I suggest a set of clothes packed in the car to change into as soon as the trip is completed so that you can be somewhat clean and dry for your drive home.

9. **Portaging:**

Carry your packs over the portage **first**. This enables you to learn the trail and remember where there are narrow planks, muddy puddles, steep hills, sharp turns, complicated hopscotch rock patterns and the trees or branches that hang low. You may not see these as well while carrying the canoe on your head.

Practice lifting and carrying a canoe before you leave home, before attempting the first actual portage. There may be many seasoned witnesses to entertain. Decide who will be the forward carrier if two are carrying the canoe.

On one canoe trip, Doug took one canoe on his own. Our younger daughter scooped up all the paddles and life jackets. My older daughter and I were to carry the second canoe. We are both fit and able, but evidently, I'm not the smart one. We raised the canoe easily and set it in place over our heads. Hurray. I ended up facing my daughter. I should have been facing forward, of course. Oh, bother. Try again. I felt so embarrassed.

Beware the tether of the Tilly hat. After completing the portage, we saw that Doug looked as though he would pass out. He had correctly placed the center canoe yoke on his shoulders, but it rested on his Tilly hat and slowly pushed it further and further back, causing the tether around his neck to become tighter and tighter. He didn't want to slow our progress on the hot portage, so he just persevered. If we had to go further, he might have passed out. Silly man.

One should never hurry down a steep, rocky hill. I'm sure you can imagine all the painful consequences of just one little slip.

10. **Etiquette or camping rules,** written and traditional.

The Provincial Park rules are:

- **Do not** bring firewood from outside the park.
- Campground campers must buy the Park's firewood, but interior campers can scavenge wood for campfire/cooking.
- **Do not** bring any tins or glass while camping in the interior.
- **Do not put any** soap into the rivers or lakes.
- While portaging, stay on the right side. Yield to oncoming canoe carriers.
- Be friendly. You never know when you may need someone's help.
- Camp only at campsite-signed locations.
- Use the thunderbox.

I have found toilet paper littering everywhere at a couple of campsites. Why? Please use the thunderbox. Toilet paper should be in the box or burned in the fire pit.

- Bring out ALL your garbage. You must bring out all that you bring in.
- Leave a pile of firewood for the next campers. Keep the campfire pit rocks piled well. Do not pile firewood right beside the fire pit. Make sure the fire is totally out before bed and before leaving the campsite.
- Keep the campsite clean and safe.
- Leave a campsite better than the way you find it. I believe this is an excellent rule to live by. Leave this world a better place than you found it.

11. Behold the beauty. Enjoy each moment.

Get out. Get free of the barriers of walls. Get away from the pavement, steel, and cement. Get out in the midst of the wilderness. Be surrounded by life. Breathe deeply the clean refreshing air. No chemicals, no toxic fumes. Get close to creation and witness the beauty, and artistry of our Creator.

Paddle the clear waters. Slow down to glide by and spy on the great blue heron. Stop to listen to the birds, search for frogs and ducks and photograph the water lilies. Even the bugs are all unique, colourful and beautiful.

Be energized by the misty sunrises. Find the treasure in the early morning light shining through the intricate, dewy spider's web.

Sunbathe on the soft, warm sandy beaches. Notice the vast variety of life and leaf, tiny fish, wildflowers and majestic ancient trees.

Be awed by the stunning sunsets.

Be still and be entertained by playful otters, the minks hurrying by the shoreline, the gigantic snapper slipping through the deep waters, and the busy beavers trying to block your travels. Just listen and try to imagine what the loons are conversing about. Be serenaded by the base bullfrog chorus. Be awestruck by the spectacular night sky's incredible infinity.

Forget about your plans for the next campsite or the next meal or even the next portage. Just enjoy the moment.

Enjoy the rhythm of the paddling strokes. Search the shoreline for all the hidden critters watching you. You may be surprised around the next bend by meeting the enormous moose.

Admire the rock formations through the clean, clear depth beneath you or the sun's artistic patterns through the water onto the sandy lake's shallow bottom.

I am blessed to have a supportive, strong, talented husband who even encourages my crazy passion for wilderness canoe camping. I am fortunate to have wonderful children who are fun-loving, nature-loving, good sports, strong canoeists, and swimmers. Even if they are just day trips, canoe trips offer an excellent venue to spend time with your children and good friends.

12. **Dare to go solo:** enjoy yourself.

Be still. Enjoy the peace, the time to think and be rejuvenated. Be inspired by the beauty of God's artistic creation. Maybe this is the best time and place to truly be still, come closer to the Creator and better experience His love.

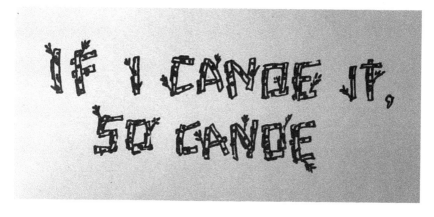

"But now ask the beasts, and they will teach you; And the birds of the air, and they will tell you;
Or speak to the earth, and it will teach you; And the fish of the sea will explain to you.
Who among all these does not know That the hand of the Lord has done this,
In whose hand is the life of every living thing, And the breath of all mankind?"
Job 12:7-10

"The earth is filled with Your love, O Lord."

Psalms 119:64